D0759487

Clark E. Moustakas

is a faculty member of the Merrill-Palmer Institute in Detroit. In addition, he is involved with other colleges and universities in workshops and seminars focusing on creativity and conformity, loneliness and individuality, child and family therapy, and human values and human learning. His other books include *Loneliness, Loneliness and Love, Creativity and Conformity, Psychotherapy With Children,* and *The Authentic Teacher.* He values being alone, being with others, and creating a full life.

Cereta Perry

is a faculty member of the Merrill-Palmer Institute, and co-leader with Clark Moustakas of the Institute's program unit *Enhancing Human Potentials in Young Children and Their Families.* She has also served on the staffs of the Counseling Center at Michigan State University, the public schools of Washington, D.C., and at Howard University. Her current interest is "Helping individuals find effective ways of developing their potentials and helping teachers, administrators, and parents create educational programs which will enable children to develop their potentials."

[clark e. moustakas ʃ cereta perry]

LEARNING TO BE FREE

A SPECTRUM BOOK

PRENTICE-HALL, INC. ENGLEWOOD CLIFFS, N.J.

Library of Congress Cataloging in Publication Data

MOUSTAKAS, CLARK E
    Learning to be free.

    (A Spectrum Book)
    "Bibliography of children's books": p.
    Bibliography: p.
    1. Education—Experimental methods: I. Perry,
Cereta. II. Title.
LB1027.M69 1973   371.3   73–7812
    ISBN 0–13–527457–5
    ISBN 0–13–527440–0 (pbk.)

For Rosa Perry Lee
cereta's mother and clark's friend,

whose valuing of the unique and special
in each of her children
and in all children
actively affirms the process of becoming

Cover photo of the authors by Donna Harris.

10 9 8 7 6 5 4 3 2 1

PRENTICE-HALL INTERNATIONAL, INC. (*London*)
PRENTICE-HALL OF AUSTRALIA PTY. LTD. (*Sydney*)
PRENTICE-HALL OF CANADA LTD. (*Toronto*)
PRENTICE-HALL OF INDIA PRIVATE LIMITED (*New Delhi*)
PRENTICE-HALL OF JAPAN, INC. (*Tokyo*)

Contents

Acknowledgments   *vii*

AWARENESS AND FREEDOM IN LEARNING   1

INVITATION AND BACKGROUND OF INVOLVEMENT   21

SELF TO SELF: *Nonverbal and Verbal Awareness*   27

SELF WITH ONE OTHER: *Partners and Pairs*   37

ENCOUNTERS IN LEARNING   50

MATHEMATICS FOR THE HUMAN CLASSROOM   81

THE PLAY-THERAPY PROGRAM   95

THE TEACHER FOR HUMANISTIC EDUCATION   109

OPEN-COMMUNICATION GROUPS:
  Joining of Community People and School Staff   128

EXTENDING THE INVITATION TO OTHERS   146

CLOSING DAYS—NEW LIFE   167

Supplemental Materials and Resources   169

Bibliography of Children's Books   171

Selected Professional Bibliography   174

Index   181

Acknowledgements

Learning To Be Free came into being as the result of the commitment, involvement, and participation of many people.

In the early days Clinton Isom, principal of the Williams School, and Ruby Williams, chairman of the Williams School Neighborhood Committee, provided the inspiration and encouragement needed to move from ideals into action.

We also want to recognize other staff members of the Williams School who have been with us through the numerous frustrations from the beginning months and have continued to help create exciting experiences for human classrooms. This group includes Helen Accra, Henrietta Davis, Addie Mae Freeman, Mike Jenkins, Maureen Lach, Jan Longton, Mildred Mahlatje, Earl Mandel, Peggy Maloney, Phyllis Massey, Elizabeth McClintic, Mary Sutton, and Gwen Williams.

A number of parent leaders in addition to supporting the overall project helped to create specific programs aimed at enriching teacher–parent relationships. We acknowledge Cynthia Christian, Ernestine Fields, Louise Jackson, Helen McCall, and Lovett Wilson.

Our students are present in many sections of *Learning To Be Free*. Those who worked with us in the first two years of the project are Tom Barrett, Paul Bedell, Nancy Boxill, Al Brown, Denise Deignan, Roger Fortman, Gail Godsey, John Grove, Angie Hunt, Marge Johnson, Barbara Kezur, Marilyn Malkin, Steven Nett, Alfonso Rodriguez, Michael Rucks, Barbara Sheedy, Karen Shelley, Ginny Sutton, Suzanne Toaspern, Carolyn Veresh, and Doris Ziemer.

Without the children in the kindergarten and primary unit of the Williams School this book would not have come into existence.

The resources, materials, and opportunities for the project were made possible through the support of the Merrill-Palmer Institute and J. William Rioux, its president.

In closing we express our heartfelt appreciation to Roseanne Ellicott and Mavis Wolfe for their patience and persistence in the typing of the manuscript.

CLARK MOUSTAKAS
CERETA PERRY

[clark moustakas]

AWARENESS AND FREEDOM IN LEARNING

MUCH OF THE DISILLUSIONMENT with education today, and specifically with schools, is the result of academic climates that are impersonal and unrelated to student interests, experiences, and needs. The basic philosophy and methods of traditional education lead to alienation of the child from himself, alienation from peers and from teachers, and alienation from society. Of all the forms of impoverishment that can be seen or felt in America, this loss of self—a sort of death-in-life—is surely the most devastating. It is the source of the discontent, rage, and violence that are everyday occurrences.

In *The Greening of America,* Charles Reich puts it this way:

Beginning with school, if not before, an individual is systematically stripped of his imagination, his creativity, his heritage, his dreams and his personal uniqueness, in order to fit him into a productive unit in a mass technological society. Instinct, feeling, and spontaneity are suppressed by overwhelming forces. As the individual is

1

drawn into the meritocracy, his working life is split from his home life, and both suffer from a lack of wholeness. Eventually, people virtually become their professions, roles, or occupations and are thenceforth strangers to themselves. Blacks long ago felt their deprivation of identity and potential for life. But white "soul" and blues are just beginning. Only a segment of youth is articulately aware that they too suffer an enforced loss of self—they too are losing the lives that could be theirs (8, p. 9).

The consequences of the fragmentation of the self are manifest in anger, frustration, insensitivity, revolt, and, finally, denial of honesty, truth, and integrity.

The only antidote to an alienating world is the development of a strong and continuing self-awareness and the freedom to learn and to be.

When awareness and freedom are central values in learning, children are introduced to wide ranges of experience. They are offered new avenues of expression and new opportunities for exploration and action. Life expands and deepens as children are free to respond, talk back, reach out to touch life, and actualize their potential:

in color—with wide variations in hue, brightness, composition

in sound—with new patterns, vibrations, and tones

in texture and touch—infinite feelings to rove over and through via a diversity of media

in ideas—sailing freely in and out of the mind; new styles of thought and expression, coming both from the child's experiences and a variety of literary sources

in tastes—aesthetic movements and appreciations coming alive through seeing, hearing, touching, feeling, conceiving, doing, creating.

Illustrative material might include: electronic equipment, cooking materials, cloth for weaving, clay for use in pottery, plastic media, paints, nuts, bolts, carpentry tools, woods, metals, machines, photographic equipment, radios, books, films, wheels, bicycle parts, toys and toy parts, odds and ends from houses and buildings, musical instruments, records, tape recorders, family and community people, books, puzzles, chalks, various types of papers—mediums already a vital part of the child's world and new outlets that could offer a primary interest and challenge.

This passage from George F. Kneller is an example of what I have in mind:

> On his way home, should he catch sight of a flock of birds gathering against a darkening sky or a burst of sunlight flaring upon a garden wall, or should he hear the cry of traffic swept far off on the evening air, he would take these impressions to his heart and let them instruct him in their obscure and tongueless way of the mystery of things. Life itself, vaster than our expression of it, speaks to us in countless ways—in the words of a friend, in the movement of a symphony, in a breath of wind across a bed of flowers, in the sight of cities, in the sirens of factories, in the murmur of pain, in the shouts of ecstasy. If our students are to be creative, let them listen to life (4).

If learning is to be an alive and vital process, the development of self-awareness is essential. Awareness involves a unity of thought and feeling, here and now; it is a necessary component in the movement toward self-actualization and toward becoming a person. In order to grow in awareness, the individual may have to stop the action, pause, and center directly on himself. What am I feeling at this moment? What is happening within me right now? What is my mood? Do I feel tensions in my body? If I listen carefully, can I actively be in touch with the source of my discontent? What do I want? What do I prefer? How many different levels of awareness can I reach when I am alone? Can I describe each feeling? What thoughts and feelings stand out? Concentrated attention and focusing are initial steps through which awareness develops. In awareness, the person is in touch immediately with inner states; he is being his real self.

Once children learn to focus, concentrate, and notice, once they are open and aware of their feelings, learning becomes exciting and unique; it becomes a personal adventure. With the child fully present as an individual, and with awareness of the immediate situation, there is also freedom from within to explore real interests and to use appropriate resources and talents. Awareness and being are inherent in the expression of creative energy and in the development of real abilities. Having the freedom to learn through preference and desire enables the child to face conflict and pain, to make mistakes, and to grow from both negative and positive experiences. Learning becomes an encounter with life, an exciting unfolding of self to self and of self to other persons. Through his expanded awareness, the child comes to discover and identify the aspects of his world that are his primary concerns—growth as a unique self, development of important relations, creation of activities and projects that have meaning and that contribute to self-esteem, finding out what capabilities are most satisfying.

The significance of self-awareness is described by Nathaniel Branden in the following excerpt:

> When a person acts without knowledge of what he thinks, feels, needs or wants, he does not yet have the option of choosing to act differently. That option comes into existence with self-awareness. That is why self-awareness is the basis of change.
>
> When a person becomes self-aware, he is in a position to acknowledge responsibility for that which he does, including that which he does to himself, to acknowledge that *he* is the cause of his actions—and thus to take ownership of his own life. Self-responsibility grows out of self-awareness.
>
> When a person becomes aware of what he is and takes responsibility for what he does, he experiences the freedom to express his authentic thoughts and feelings, to express his authentic self. Self-assertiveness becomes possible with the achievement of self-awareness and the acknowledgement of self-responsibility (*1*, p. 171).

The child who is aware of himself is ready to venture into known and unknown paths. As he feels freedom from within, he can risk, he can experiment, try out potentials and resources until he discovers satisfying and rewarding projects to pursue. Then he enters the learning situation in a sustained and fulfilling way. The child who is free and acts on his preferences is willing to immerse himself in experience, to enter the world of nature, of science, literature, or art and remain alive in his learning. He can savor, enjoy, digest, relate, discover, and ultimately integrate in himself sources of life that are available to him in the school and outside. He can take an unpredictable journey in painting, in drawing, in music, in dance, in literature; even math can become a valued learning experience. With awareness and freedom to act on his own preferences, he is open to everything about him: he feels his own body alive in action; he trusts the value of his choices or alters them to fit the rhythm of his experience. He is open to touch, to smell, to taste, to life.

Since self-awareness is the first step toward genuine, enduring learning, it is essential that schools and families create projects and activities that recognize the immediate concerns and feelings of the child. Meditation, poetry, focusing on the feeling of experiences, and discussions aimed at revealing sadness, loneliness, pain, joy, anger, fear, and love are necessary ways to authentic self-development. Intuition and mystery should be treated with the respect given more concrete and tangible forms of reality.

Once the conditions of freedom and awareness are met, three values become important in the growth of the self and the formation of real connections with others. The most fundamental of these values is *commitment*. Unless the child uses his awareness and freedom to make choices that involve authentic challenges and concerns, his development stays on the surface and remains temporary and fragmented; his development is based on fancy and whim, on the attractive and sensational, on escapism rather than on deep-rooted and fundamental issues. The commitment of the child to what he is engaged in, when it represents an honest pursuit, ensures that he will stay with the project or problem long enough to achieve a full knowing of the situation. This means bringing to life energies, resources, and talents, and a willingness to struggle to a point of resolution. For example, the desire to play a guitar, even when based on freedom and awareness rather than expectation or demand, is not enough to ensure satisfactory experience. The commitment of the child is essential if he is to find out whether he is actually interested and whether his potential is sufficient to lead to a sense of fulfillment. To answer the question of fit requires a staying with the problem or challenge, working on it, exerting oneself and struggling, doing everything necessary to develop fluency and competence.

Commitment means that the child is determined to put himself into all the necessary moments and to find from within his own experience the answer to whether he will be a guitar player. If he gives up before he has faced all the requirements of real learning, he will never know. True commitment means staying with a process until it has been fully experienced. It is then possible to make a judgment of yes or no. Even when a decision turns out to have been a bad choice, the experience has not been wasted. What the individual hoped for, dreamed about, and imagined did not happen, but growth is taking place in other ways. Learning through error is a way to awareness, and a way to knowing oneself.

A second value in genuine learning is the *involvement* of the child. He must be in his learning as a self, fully alive and present, staying awake to his own feelings while also being in touch with others. Involvement includes a sense of caring. He feels that what he has to offer is essential not only to himself but also to others; he feels the value of others. Involvement is expressed in a sense of responsibility, in a concern not just for the process of learning but also for the outcomes. The involved person pursues his own interests, but he also helps others to develop what is important to them. Involvement—in attitude, in presence, in behavior—means a willingness and a determination to create experiences for oneself and with others that keep life moving in significant ways.

A third value in real learning is the *active participation* of the learner. Participation on an active basis means a willingness to share, to openly explore with others, in verbal and in nonverbal communications. Active participation at its highest level includes the initiation of projects, the opening of issues, and the direct pursuit of problems, interests, concerns. Participation may take the form of *reactions* to nature, materials, or other persons, or it may take the form of *response*. A *reaction* is an explanation, an interpretation, an analysis, a reflection or a paraphrase; it is other-directed communication: "What you are saying is that you are angry with your mother." "Bill, when you talk like that, you don't have any regard for anyone else." "Jill, the truth is that you are lazy." In reaction, the focus is on the other; in response the focus is on the self. A *response* is an expression of one's own inner experience, a direct expression of feeling: "I am angry," "I am frightened," "I love you." A reaction is one of a series of associations. *A* makes a comment; *B* associates his own comment to it; this is followed by *C*. Thus, a reaction is a link in a chain; it is not complete in itself. A response, on the other hand, is complete in itself. It does not require additions; it is total. A reaction is "if," "but," "when." A response is "yes" or "no," "this" or "that." It is person-to-person communication.

Genuine learning and growth are self-initiated responses to life, expressions of one's own voice, inner experience, desire, preference, feeling. Whether the individual initiates communication or is responding to another, the message is always personal, internal, descriptive and characteristic of the child himself. True learning, then, is initiative and responsive, not reactive. True learning reflects the self of the learner, not the self of the other. In a relationship, the persons are mutually responsive. Reactions are helpful in seeking information and in gathering facts, but they do not contribute to personal enhancement or to life. Thus, teachers should encourage children to initiate and determine their own learning and to respond with whatever feelings and thoughts are evoked. Practice in initiating and in responding is essential to the development of the self and to learning that is meaningful, exciting, and rewarding.

Silence may be a response or it may be a reaction. As a response, silence contributes to a sense of community. It strengthens, affirms, adds an important dimension. As a reaction, silence diminishes, frustrates, blocks, and even distorts, or it may simply be innocuous, noncontributing, empty. Silence can enhance or it can detract. At times the individual must break his silence and verbally communicate what he is experiencing. Only in this way can he stand out in real-life form; only in this way can he have an impact, can he affect life.

Genuine learning and growing, whether in one's own self or with one other person or in a group, require awareness and the freedom to be. Once these conditions are present it is essential that the child commit himself on the basis of his own desires and preferences and that he actively participate in life both as an initiator and in response, in solitary projects and activities and in joint efforts and communications. The commitment, involvement, and active participation of the child make the difference between a real process of learning and the motions of learning that typify too many school activities.

As long as the individual remains in touch with himself and lives in accordance with his own awareness and preferences, he will continue to be what he can be, develop along the lines of his potential, remain true to his biological makeup. When he loses touch with his personal possibilities, he falls short of his potential; his world becomes narrower and more constricted. Maslow cites the neurotic consequences:

> I think for instance of the fine pianist who couldn't play before an audience of more than a few, or the phobic who is forced to avoid heights or crowds. The person who can't study, or who can't sleep, or who can't eat many foods has been diminished as surely as the one who has been blinded. The cognitive losses, the lost pleasures, joys, and ecstasies, the loss of competence, the inability to relax, the weakening of will, the fear of responsibility—all these are diminutions of humanness (5, pp. 33–34).

Much in present-day school life contributes to a neurotic process, especially when the child is treated as an object of learning to be molded, shaped, prodded, pushed, and then rewarded or punished. Whenever lessons are dictated and imposed, whenever a child is classified and labeled, whenever he is plotted on a chart and compared, his uniqueness is being violated and he is forced to either take a path of conformity or to go underground. Rather than making learning an act of discovery and a pursuit based on interest and relevance, too many teachers are frozen people who are so busy manipulating and imposing that they have lost touch with the real world of childhood, which O'Gorman describes in the following passage from his book, *The Storefront*.

> Childhood is a gift the gods give children. It is as precious as the rubies they give the earth and the sun they give the spheres. It is each child's absolutely; as rare as a unicorn or a phoenix. One

childhood to every child. No two childhoods are alike. Childhood is the form that upholds each child's life forever. If a man or a society taints a child's childhood, brutalizes it, strikes it down, and corrupts it with fear and bad dreams, then he maims that child forever, and the judgment on that man and that society will be terrible and eternal (7, pp. 3–4).

When the child is treated as an object of learning, as an incomplete thing, as an empty vessel to be filled with facts and explanations, his only chance, if he is to survive as a person, is to rebel. He must use his energies to fight or live continually in a dishonest state. His alienation not only relates to the external world but also enters inside and erodes the child's energy and spirit. He loses touch with his own awareness of what is important and what is real. Then his goal becomes one of defeating the teacher's efforts and ambitions; energies are used to block and restrain rather than to grow.

Kneller has pointed out the deadening effect of the teacher who, in an effort to become organized and meet the bureaucratic demands of the system, has made the values of the system prominent:

> In the schools creative energy is frustrated by regulations designed to keep masses of young people in order by making them behave in unison. It is frustrated, too, by tired, overworked teachers, who cannot spare the time to nurture the creativity of the individual student because they must struggle amid the impersonal web of administrative detail and mass guidance and counseling procedures to instill into their swollen classes the basic requirements of a stereotyped syllabus (4, p. 99).

When learning is divorced from human values, the persons involved in the process are alienated from each other and from themselves. The child engages in activities that have nothing to do with his own integrity, with his own response to life. He is alienated from the teacher, who does not exist as a person, who does not recognize his uniqueness, and does not know that reality is based on freedom, awareness, commitment, involvement, and active participation, and not on external assignments, purposes, motives, and goals. Eventually, when the child is denied as a self, his own feelings become blunted; his wishes are cut off and rejected as a basis for learning; his sensitivity and awareness are defeated through criticism, through the imposition of external standards of conformity, and through authoritarian modes of group life. Finally, he becomes fragmented in the labels and classifications applied to him. Or, he stands firm in the face of alienation and denial. His rebellion may be active when he remains in the center and makes the classroom an arena for fighting and violence, or it may take a passive and resistant form.

What are some of the ways used in the family and in the school to manipulate children, to impose and enforce external standards and values? What are the ways that eventually lead to submission, conformity and alienation?

ROLE PLAYING AND SUBMISSION TO THE PECKING ORDER

Here the child is forced to find his place in the hierarchy and stay in it. In the family, he is assigned certain characteristics, tasks, and appropriate behavior. In the school he is labeled and classified, put into a hierarchy, assigned a place, defined as a learner. He is told that certain acts are appropriate, and that he must learn how and when to carry these out. He comes to know in advance the reward or punishment that will follow each act. From an early age he is able to perceive how he is defined by parents at home and by teachers in school. Thus, the self-fulfilling prophecy is at work. If he is defined as a slow learner he learns to act like one. Whenever he acts out the definitions and expectations of others, he is going against himself. The higher up he goes in status, power, and prestige, the more complicated is his impersonation, the more dishonest he becomes. Such a person is not aware of who he really is and does not know what he can do; he no longer knows what is true for him. The role player is other-directed. He has no real opportunity to develop an identity of his own. In playing a role, whatever that role may be, the individual gives up something of himself. The more the role takes over his entire being, the more total is his alienation.

THE I-IT PROCESS

Any situation in which the child is treated as an object, as an "it" or a thing, contributes to his alienation. When we observe, examine, take notes on, and in other ways externalize the individual, we are fragmenting him and separating him from life. When we pressure the child to perceive on the basis of facts imposed from without, rather than from the unity of his experience, we engage in an I-It process. Labeling and classifying encourage splintering and narrowing of the self.

Double messages—saying one thing but meaning another—manipulation, the use of indirect and devious methods, discrepancy between behavior and feeling, failure to listen and actually hear, rejection of the real self, treating what the person communicates as data for analysis, explanation, and questioning: all remove the child from himself and interfere with his own awareness of the essentials in living and learning. When a creative process is interrupted by rules, demands, and schedules, the individual loses contact with real life and enters into object-to-object communication, the lowest point being manifested in mechanical and routinized behavior.

In the beginning, self-to-self communication is the natural means of expression, but through manipulation and alienation the self loses its ability to focus and center, and relationships deteriorate into object-to-object communication. Buber writes: "The primary word *I-It* is not of evil—as matter is not of evil. It is of evil—as matter is, which presumes to have the quality of present being. If a man lets it have the mastery, the continually growing world of *It* overruns him and robs him of the reality of his own I, till the incubus over him and the ghost within him whisper to one another the confession of their non-salvation" (2, p. 46).

Of course, in the process of alienating the child by using I-It forms of communication, the teacher or other authority figure becomes increasingly alienated from himself and more firmly entrenched in his role.

EVALUATION

Evaluation tactics put teeth into organization and control of life in the home and in the school. Evaluations are forms of conditioning, rewarding the "appropriate" and punishing the "inappropriate." Since the child as a whole is always unique and cannot actually be evaluated, the parts become the focus of attention. Objects have parts that can be defined, judged, and evaluated, but persons are unified wholes. Thus, evaluation can be directed only at traits or specific characteristics. In an evaluation process, the value of the child is eliminated, since his value—that is, his uniqueness—cannot be judged, compared, or rated. To avoid being rejected, disapproved of, and denied opportunities, the individual submits, gives up his individuality and wholeness. Evaluation would not be effective if consequences did not follow that remove human rights and thwart and close doors. Judging, grading, and other forms of reward and punishment are effective deterrents to personal growth. Soon the child begins to look outside to find out whether his expressions and productions are good. He learns to judge himself and the value of what he does by other people's judgments and ratings. When the individual and the object he makes become one, the evaluation process has been successful. It has forced him to give himself up. He becomes his products; his products determine his worth. Thus the good reader becomes the good person. Production and efficiency rather than uniqueness and creativity determine the value of what the person does. Ultimately, through continual evaluation, the individual learns to wear different masks and to play different roles to satisfy the experts and authorities who have the power to affect his life.

A high school class in East Orange, New Jersey, listed the following as most characteristic of their reactions to the evaluative system:

We have all kinds of pressures.
People are always telling us what to do.
We have to take courses that have no meaning to us.
Adults tell us to decide, and then they don't like the decision.
We're not all the same—there are different points of view among us.
We want to move without too many restrictions.
We want to become more aware of things by ourselves.
Even though things are complicated, we're still enthusiastic.
Adults want us to conform, and so we lose our identity.
We have to conform to the group, so our friends will like us.
We have to have good ideas to be somebody.

(11, p. 154)

ACCOUNTABILITY

This is another name for evaluation with extra threats thrown in. If certain conditions are not met by the teachers themselves, consequences such as dismissal, denial of promotion, and pay cuts will occur. Accountability is set up to evaluate people who have gone up the ladder and have found a secure and safe spot. It is meant to remove the security. The individual has arrived at a place where he sometimes evaluates and judges others, but clever administrators and politicians have devised a new scheme for evaluating the evaluators. Thus, for example, teachers are held "accountable" and evaluated by their peers and higher-ups, and sometimes by the students themselves.

In contrast to procedures and ways that alienate and diminish is the process of I-Thou—of genuine encounter.

THE I-THOU PROCESS—THE ENCOUNTER PROCESS

The only way to avoid playing roles and wearing masks, the only way to thwart the I-It process, is to remain in touch with oneself, to be aware of one's own values, interests, and concerns, to know what one prefers, and to act consistently on these values and preferences. By maintaining contact, the I of the person becomes formulated into an identity, into a real self that can meet and encounter other real selves. Buber expresses it this way:

> When *Thou* is spoken, the speaker has no thing for his object. For where there is a thing there is another thing. Every *It* is bounded by others; *It* exists only through being bounded by others. But when *Thou* is spoken, there is no thing. *Thou* has no bounds. . . .
>
> I consider a tree.
>
> I can look on it as a picture: stiff column in a shock of light, or splash of green shot with the delicate blue and silver of the background.
>
> I can perceive it as movement: flowing veins on clinging, pressing pith, suck of the roots, breathing of the leaves, ceaseless commerce with earth and air—and the obscure growth itself.
>
> I can classify it in a species and study it as a type in its structure and mode of life. . . .
>
> It can, however, also come about, if I have both will and grace, that in considering the tree I become bound up in relation to it. The tree is now no longer It. I have been seized by the power of exclusiveness.
>
> To effect this it is not necessary for me to give up any of the ways in which I consider the tree. There is nothing from which I would have to turn my eyes away in order to see, and no knowledge that I would have to forget. Rather is everything, picture and movement, species and type, law and number, indivisibly united in this event.
>
> Everything belonging to the tree is in this: its form and structure, its colours and chemical composition, its intercourse with the elements and with the stars, are all present in a single whole. . . . I encounter no soul or dryad of the tree, but the tree itself (2, pp. 7–8).*

The encounter process is a sharing of oneself while being fully with the other person. It involves presence, actuality, listening, hearing, an awareness of the immediate, of a sense of mutuality. It is a

* Quotation from *I and Thou*, by Martin Buber, copyright © 1958 by Charles Scribner's Sons. Reprinted by permission of Charles Scribner's Sons and T. & T. Clark, Edinburgh.

commitment that goes all the way. Two qualities often part of this process are *grooving* and *groking*. Starche has effectively described how grooving on life is zeroing in on it, focusing on it fully, concentrating on it, putting oneself fully into it, knowing it. To grok in learning is to know the situation from all its levels, to see it and comprehend it, both spiritually and physically, to experience it, identify it, and, above all, to discern what it is for. Groking involves an inner journey—going into oneself to fully grok another person or situation, and then acting on it through direct encounter.

Learning that is real inevitably involves a struggle with oneself and with life. Monotonous repetition, memorization, testing and evaluation do not bring life, they merely transmit bad faith. Under the guise of scientific proof of achievement, these procedures undermine uniqueness, individuality, and personal integrity by promoting sameness, uniformity, and a closed system in which life is based on external authoritarian standards and guided by rules and regulations defining what is appropriate and of value.

Rather than simply reinforcing preconceived notions of what should be learned, the adult can be open to new experience and, being open himself, can encourage the child to attune himself to the intuition of his own senses—the breathing of the leaves; the sound of his own footsteps; the movement of the clouds; the rhythm of his body in motion; the pain and suffering of his neighbor; the joy and wonder of discovery; the response to texture, smell, color; the experience of tears and laughter; the beauty and excitement of a new idea. Life is contained in the words of a real friend, in the pain of defeat and accident, in the agony of conflict and of love, in the excitement of play, in the search for the solution to real problems.

In human education the subject matter is related to the learner and stems from his own innovations, interests, and commitments. Genuine education is not something out there, existing in fragments and pieces, but is within the person's own capacities, talents, and preferences. It is his encounters with life that inspire, motivate, involve, enable, and encourage the person to search, inquire, and deepen his knowledge and interest. Genuine resources of learning are not objects in the minds of adults to be used to "motivate," compel, and vanquish the learner through either the manipulation of reward and punishment or the manipulation of "love" and power. Genuine learning does not consist of a programmed course of study to be memorized and repeated but rather it comes from raw material, from life itself. When truly relevant to a child, a book is not merely a book but is a source of encounter and relatedness, a source of life. So, too, with maps, movies, instruments, sounds, smells, colors, shapes, forms, water, earth, sky, people, trees, motions, mechanics, air—with any dimension of the world that captivates the individual, sustains him as a human being and enables him to grow. Any subject matter or environmental resource that extends knowledge, deepens appreciation and understanding, and expands the awareness of the learner is an appropriate source. Hawkins' description of the curriculum characterizing the creative kindergarten of the "progressive education" era relates the kind of subject matter and life experience that can be engendered in the modern school:

> Here there was not only a style of teaching that involved children deeply in subject matter, but the subject matter grew with the style—water, sand, clay, paint, good infant literature, the cultivation of story and song, carpentry, lenses, prisms, magnets, blocks, the house of packing boxes and orange crates, soil and seeds, animals, the dance, and all the rest. I do not believe that this tradition failed at all; its influence has been reduced by erosion (sometimes to the vanishing point), by pressures for thin mechanical programs of "reading readiness," "number experience," and the like, most of which tend to reduce the very readiness they seek to cultivate (3, p. 547).

In his book *Freedom To Learn*, Carl Rogers discusses a number of ways through which the teacher can foster freedom and authentic learning in the classroom. Some of his suggestions, in modified form, follow:

1. *Building upon problems perceived as real.* Confrontation by a real problem is an essential condition of genuine learning. This applies whether we refer to a small child desiring to make change, a young person struggling to construct a stereo set, a college student formulating his views on racial problems, the fear of a young teacher-in-training conducting a first practice

session, or the adult dealing with interpersonal relations or marital problems.

2. *Providing resources.* The teacher brings to the classroom all those resources which are believed to contribute to important learning in reading, numbers, science, literature, art, music, and dance.

3. *Using contracts.* This method provides a transitional experience between complete freedom to learn whatever is of interest, and learning that is relatively free but still within the limits of some institutional demand. The teacher and the child agree on a timetable of lessons, projects, and activities. Some of these are initiated, sponsored, or desired by the teacher, and some by the child. Both enter the contract in good faith and are expected to fulfill its terms.

4. *Dividing a group.* When a group is offered freedom to learn, there should be provision for those who do not wish or desire this freedom and prefer to be instructed or guided. For example, learning can be made available for those children who want to learn sequentially, step by step, and who want to be guided by experts. The teacher can work with these children in traditional ways in those areas where this approach is preferred.

5. *Forming learning groups.* Here the children are divided into interest groups or groups pursuing specific issues and problems in learning. The teacher and student-leaders serve as facilitators in discussions. These groups are formed to set up projects aimed at expanding knowledge and skill, and engage in activities that will make life in the classroom a rich learning experience.

6. *Posing problems.* Possession of a body of knowledge *about* science is not adequate achievement today. The student must get away from the image of science as an absolute, complete, and permanent system. To strengthen the autonomous processes within the child, special training is needed for teachers of science. The teacher sets the stage of inquiry by posing problems, creating an environment responsive to the learner, and giving assistance in the investigative operations. Then students can engage in self-directed learning and make discoveries themselves. They become scientists on a simple level, seeking an-

swers to real questions, learning the pitfalls and the joys of the scientist's search.

7. *Involving the child in experiential learning.* "A 'simulation' is a social system in miniature; a model of an organization, a nation, or a world—a 'laboratory analogue' by which a wide variety of social situations can be replicated. . . ." Simulation experiences offer the student an opportunity for direct involvement with processes that occur in real life, such as decision-making based upon incomplete and changing information, difficulties in communication, and the handling of interpersonal relationships in situations requiring negotiation, bargaining, and compromise. In these experiences, the student is responsible for his decisions and actions. He learns to gather information, sift it through, and determine a course of action, thus developing a positive and constructive type of learning attitude.

8. *Using programmed instruction.* Sometimes in the process of learning, the student becomes aware of gaps in his knowledge, of tools he is lacking, or of information needed to deal with a problem he is confronting. In these instances programmed instruction is often a more efficient guide than the classroom teacher. A student who wants to learn how to use a microscope can find a program covering this knowledge. A student planning to visit France can utilize programmed instruction in conversational French, and one needing algebra, whether for solving a specific problem or simply to meet a college requirement, can also locate a guided program of instruction in that area.

9. *Creating encounter groups.* In these groups little structure is imposed and members of the group are encouraged to make decisions and create their own experiences. The focus is on issues and problems in relationships and in communication. The leader facilitates communication and clarifies or points up the pattern of the group's struggle to work toward a meaningful experience. In such a group, after an initial exploratory phase, personal expressiveness increases. Façades become less necessary, defenses are lowered, and basic encounters occur as individuals share feelings and aspects of themselves. Spontaneous feedback—both negative and positive—is given by group members. Eventually, there is greater freedom of expression of

each individual, and the group as a whole develops a sense of community.

10. *Permitting self-evaluation.* The teacher does not assign readings, impose lesson plans, lecture, or expound. He does not evaluate and criticize unless a student wishes his judgment. He does not give examinations or take sole responsibility for grades. He permits the learner to determine his own guidelines for judging the value of what he is learning and how well he is learning.

In summary, the real world of the learner is a world of personal meaning and involvement, a world centered in the self, where interests, activities, and concerns take on individual forms peculiar to each child. Although it is important for the instructor to meet the child on the intellectual and cognitive level, it is much more important to meet him on his most human level and to keep open the doors of communication and of human relations. It is more important to keep values in the forefront in learning. In no way should human values be neglected. Sensitivity, awareness, uniqueness, responsiveness, respect for the integrity of the learner and his preferences and interests, authenticity, honesty, truth, love: each has its place in everyday meetings and each is more important than the most important fact or skill. In no way should expediency, efficiency, organization, and achievement push the self of the learner away, for the self of the learner is his one unique contribution to humanity, his one tie to meaning and to life.

REFERENCES

1. Branden, Nathaniel. *The Disowned Self.* Los Angeles: Nash, 1971.
2. Buber, Martin. *I and Thou.* Trans. by Ronald Gregor Smith. Edinburgh: T. & T. Clark, 1937.
3. Hawkins, David. *The Informed Vision: An Essay on Science Education. Daedalus,* Summer 1965, vol. 94, no. 3, pp. 538–52.
4. Kneller, George F. *The Art and Science of Creativity.* New York: Holt, Rinehart & Winston, 1965.

5. Maslow, Abraham H. *The Farther Reaches of Human Nature.* New York: Viking, 1971.

6. Moustakas, Clark. *The Authentic Teacher: Sensitivity and Awareness in the Classroom.* Cambridge, Mass.: Howard A. Doyle, 1966.

7. O'Gorman, Ned. *The Storefront.* New York: Harper & Row, 1970.

8. Reich, Charles A. *The Greening of America.* New York: Random House, 1970.

9. Rogers, Carl R. *Freedom To Learn.* Columbus, Ohio: Charles Merrill, 1969.

10. Starche, Walter. *The Ultimate Revolution.* New York: Harper & Row, 1969.

11. Weinstein, Gerald and Fantini, Mario D. (Eds.) *Toward Humanistic Education.* New York: Praeger, 1970.

12. Yashima, Taro. *Crow Boy.* New York: Viking, 1955.

[cereta perry]

INVITATION AND BACKGROUND OF INVOLVEMENT

OUR "HUMAN CLASSROOM" PROJECT in inner-city Detroit schools began with an invitation from a group of parents representing the Williams School Neighborhood Committee (WSNC). A summary of one of their meetings was contained in their letter to us:

> During this meeting we discussed the possibility of developing a working relationship between Merrill-Palmer and the Williams School. We talked about such things as setting up some type of class or workshop for parents on Family Life and Child Development; working with teachers and aides on sensitivity training or a workshop on attitudes; having Merrill-Palmer students work directly in the classrooms; working with our teacher-counselor; working with 25 students who, during the past school year, while in the kindergarten, scored A or better on the Cognitive Abilities Test; sharing with us and the school staff the results of some of your research findings.

The sincerity and urgency of the parents' request moved us to immediate action. A series of meetings was conducted with community representatives, school administrators, and the teaching staff of the Williams School.

The parent group was questioning, among other things, the effects of cultural-deprivation theory and stereotypes on the development of their children's attitudes and learning skills. The issues were similar to those voiced by Doxey Wilkerson in a recent publication:

> . . . children from the ghetto are perceived as sharing a common set of characteristics, much as if they came from the same mold. The literature on compensatory education repeatedly asserts that "these children" come from impoverished backgrounds which afford little opportunity for intellectual development—broken homes, uneducated parents or guardians with no concern for the education of their children, no books or newspapers, narrow and barren environmental settings, and the like. Consequently, they enter school largely "nonverbal," with atrocious language patterns and lacking the experiential basis for effective cognitive development. It is said, further, that their learning style is motor rather than verbal, concrete rather than abstract; that they have little or no future orientation, but seek immediate gratifications; and that their aspiration level is low and their academic motivation about nil.
>
> There is much wrong with this description, including demonstrable factual errors. However, the main weakness is that it stereotypes; it obscures the reality of human variation. Poverty is a common bond, but the "poor" are still a heterogeneous population. There are intact families, as well as broken homes; upwardly mobile families, as well as those hopelessly mired in dependency; nuclear and extended families which provide love and security and encourage educational development, as well as families whose impact on the young is mainly negative. And ghetto children, like all children, are wondrously varied human beings—in self-concept, interpersonal relations, academic ability, motivation and probable future. To perceive these children in terms of a derogatory stereotype tends not only to thwart theoretical clarity, but also to promote pedantic and sterile educational practices.[1]

[1] Sheldon Marcus and Harry Rivlin (Eds.), *Conflicts in Urban Education* (New York: Basic Books, 1970), pp. 27–29.

Excerpted from Chapter 2, "Compensatory Education," by Doxey A. Wilkerson. © 1970 by Basic Books, Inc., Publishers, New York. Reprinted by permission of the publisher.

As we met with the WSNC group, it became clear that the parents and neighborhood leaders, in addition to concerns related to the school, faced a much bigger problem—that of assimilating the culturally heterogeneous factions of their community.

The Williams School is in the central core of Detroit, marked by many signs of decay and obsolescence. Although some homes in the area are well constructed and maintained, many require repairs and improvements; and others have deteriorated to the point of being slum dwellings. Many vacant buildings are boarded up and create a depressed appearance in the community.

The population is mobile, with a strong transient element. The residents are predominantly black although other minority families live in the community. Some are longtime dwellers who have become urbanized and are either middle class or middle class in orientation. Others are newcomers from the rural south. Many residents have little formal schooling but nearly all of them have much pride in cultural traditions and customs which they practice with a great deal of satisfaction. Because of the tremendous differences in background experiences, values, and life-styles, the community is faced with the tremendous task of helping people value their neighborhood and develop an interest in unifying their resources and energies toward increased opportunities and services to children, youth, and families.

The courage, stamina, and perseverance of the WSNC has been remarkable. Consistently, the committee has attempted to assimilate the various factions of the community. Even though the total number to be reached represented an enormous task, the neighborhood leaders accepted our suggestion that working with small groups ultimately would be a more effective way of promoting unity than massive efforts and demonstrations.

A second major task of the WSNC was that of reaching the most troubled children of the school. It was decided to try to reach the parents of these children. Eventually the WSNC was successful in assembling a working group of twenty-five people: twelve "difficult to reach" parents, eight members of the WSNC, the principal and assistant principal, the community school agent, a teacher, and a psychologist from the Merrill-Palmer Institute. A series of meetings was planned on the theme "Some Ways of Helping Children Develop Effective Behaviors." The meetings were unstructured and open-ended in order to encourage maximum participation and involvement. It was clear that the pressures of daily living were so great for most of these parents that they did not feel free enough to be involved in the lives of their children in significant ways.

Another area of early involvement was the interaction with administrative and teaching staffs. Initial meetings with the principal of the school occurred almost simultaneously with meetings with the president of the WSNC. The principal had close, frequent contact with the WSNC and was aware of the efforts of this group to promote human values in the school. In response to the question "In what areas do you see Merrill-Palmer providing help?" the principal supported the goals of the WSNC and suggested that we attend and participate in his regular faculty meetings.

In the initial faculty meeting, I shared my thoughts regarding the development of human classrooms and the function of administrators, teachers, and parents in facilitating significant learning. Some teachers were ambivalent and wondered if children learn academic content in a free classroom. Other teachers were excited about the possibility of creating a new learning environment responsive to the needs and interests of children. A workshop was planned to allow for further exploration of the ideas.

The participants in the workshop included administrators, teachers, paraprofessionals, and representatives from the community. The theme was "Helping Adults Face Themselves." The workshop participants were organized into small groups and asked to determine their objectives for the week.

The following represented their major concerns: (1) improving the relationship between the school and the community; (2) achieving real parental involvement; (3) lessening the distance between the school staff and the parents and (4) maintaining discipline.

The dialogue in the small groups enabled individuals to develop an awareness, understanding, and respect for themselves and others. The comments below summarize the value of the workshop as expressed by two of the participants.

I feel that this workshop was one of the most important events ever to take place in this school. If we are to grow—to change—to help children, we must first look at ourselves. We cannot expect our children to be honest with us unless we are honest with them. I believe that a number of ideas which were brought up were threatening because many of us feel insecure and are not used to examining our feelings and actions. That there was resistance or lack of discussion when some sensitive issues were presented indicates where we are and how much more facing ourselves we need. To be free to speak honestly will take more time. We must develop the courage to be more open and the patience to try. It is my hope that Merrill-Palmer will help us discover ourselves and our relationships to one another and to the children.

It is my personal feeling that the workshop has created a friendlier atmosphere at the Williams School. I learned a great deal. I was glad to see many issues brought up. I can breathe a sigh of relief because this one workshop is not the end of our "search for truth," but rather is only a beginning. I am eager to continue.

Currently there is much rhetoric that seems to express concern for people in the inner city. Often, the genuineness of this concern is questionable because a basic element of human relations is missing—namely, respect for the dignity of the person as an individual. The very use of the term "inner city" often carries with it ugly stereotypes of educational retardation, lack of interest, lack of ability, laziness, shiftlessness, dullness.

An exciting lesson relating to the dignity of the child was brought home to me in a Salvation Army summer camp in Butler, New Jersey. The incident occurred during the fifties, well before the "war on poverty," before children were labeled "culturally deprived," before the rhetoric about proper ways of dealing with slum children, and before Harlem and New York's Lower East Side became known as the inner city.

The experience involved two hundred and twelve boys ranging in age from six to fourteen years and representing the whole spectrum of races, creeds, and national origins. They were alike in that they all lived in Harlem or on New York's Lower East Side. The Salvation Army was offering these youngsters an opportunity to experience and enjoy an out-of-doors life. I was hired as a program director to outline activities that would contribute to the enjoyment of nature and recreation. My immediate impulse was to organize a program of daily events and place the boys into assigned groups. But when I met the camp director, the message was clear: "We don't tell our children they must do anything."

After a little more interaction with her and a great deal of struggle with myself, I knew what she really meant: "We have a group of little boys coming to camp to enjoy a stay away from the city. Our children are not to be controlled or directed but they are to be respected as human beings capable of making decisions for themselves."

I discarded my notion of organized plans and began to create a program that valued free choice. It was wonderful to witness the joy and sense of worth that each boy experienced as he chose a program of activities that fit his own interests, purposes, and desires.

Additional expression of the camp director's respect for the dignity of the child was the type of orientation given the staff before the arrival of the children. We were told that the children would be expecting kind, loving, and considerate treatment. It was emphasized that these children came from homes where there was not much money but this did not mean that there was not much love; in fact, in some cases we were told, "there is not much more than love."

This experience in a camp setting again and again mirrored respect for the dignity of the individual. The principle continues to be crucial in any setting where real growth of persons is paramount.

Teachers must actively express their valuing of children's dignity so that children feel it; telling them is not sufficient. As a child experiences respect for his dignity, he begins to express himself in creative ways. When a child's creative potential is released, he moves in the direction of becoming the unique person he is capable of becoming. All children are potentially creative; they have the dynamic force which enables them to achieve many of their dreams. The development of the creative potential depends upon the child's experiences, his opportunities for self-expression, and the affirmation he receives as he expresses himself.

[clark moustakas]

SELF TO SELF
Nonverbal and Verbal Awareness

WE MET IN OPEN SPACES in a converted kindergarten and lunch-room—approximately three hundred children and thirteen adults—touching, feeling, moving, speaking, each coming to know himself, each becoming aware of dreams, of sadness, joy, anger, of moments that had been stopped, feelings that had been denied and suppressed, fears that still lived inside: fears of being rejected, of being hurt, of being humanly crushed. Gradually, we learned to express our feelings, to be who we are.

At first, we experienced chaos, confusion, wild movements, giggles, discomfort, anxiety in being alone, in becoming aware. What was this place? Who were these grown-up people who talked about learning to be free, learning to value the very special person that you are?

"Take off your shoes," someone said. "Sit quietly and hold hands." Another order! Oh, no! But wait, the voice wasn't pushing and controlling! In small groups we sat on the floor and, slowly, we removed our shoes, closed our eyes, and held hands. We were in a big world with more space than we had known in our crowded school. This world, this space, this spot in which we sat, came to be our own unique room as we met week after week. It came to be the central time and place in our lives.

At first, holding hands created a cautious feeling; we had not touched in this way before, in school, but after a few times it came to be a good feeling. Sometimes we felt restless, agitated, wiggling, full of tensions when we arrived, but in a short time it was possible to relax and be at home with ourselves. To be alone and to be aware of moment-to-moment feelings was sometimes scary, but after a while it came to feel good; it came to feel peaceful.

The person talking to us, giving us instructions, seemed to be a teacher, and yet she was not a teacher. There was something direct, warm, personal in her voice. She was speaking to many at once and yet she seemed to be speaking to me privately, to me alone. "Today we're going to learn to be with a very special person. We're going to come to know that person, to be aware that that very special person is you. It is important now to keep your eyes closed and pay attention to what it is like, what it feels like to be you. No one ever before has been just like you. You are unique, different from anyone else in all the world."

So we closed our eyes and lay on our backs, as we were instructed to do. At first, the tile floor felt hard and cold, but as the silence continued, the warmth of hands we held and bodies we touched raised our temperatures and after a while it was a pleasant sensation to rest quietly, so much so that some of us got drowsy. There was no hurry, no rush to get busy with school chores. There was a feeling that we were being guided by internal states, not by schedules and clocks.

The voice continued: "As you lie quietly be aware of your body touching the hard floor. Feel your head and shoulders; notice the weight of your arms and legs. Let your back and bottom rest comfortably. Can you hear your breathing? Take in a big gulp of air, hold it. Now let it out slowly. Do this many times."

It was hard to keep awake now. The voice was soothing. The

floor became warmer and warmer. It was a good feeling to shut my eyes and relax. I became aware of the space in which I rested. For a while I wanted to see what others were doing and I opened my eyes from time to time, but then my drowsy feeling, the lilting quality of the voice, my steady breathing, and the good feeling in my body took over. I was home, thinking of the mystery of what we were doing and yet how much I'd rather be here than back in my classroom, rushing, being pushed, working all the time, bored. I should be sleeping by now, yet more and more I was coming awake. I am aware right at this moment of the huge silence in the room, even with the immense breathing sounds. It seems quieter than if there were no sounds at all.

"Now I would like you to know the space surrounding you. You're here in your own place in this room. You'll be here many times again. Move your arms freely, touch the space all around you. Stretch as far as you can. See how far out you can go." It seemed silly to me but it was better than the classwork that didn't make sense at all. The space on my right is limited. I'm touching someone now. Was that an arm or leg or what? My left space is tight, too. But I can go way up with one arm and then the other. Now both. I'm waking up more and more. It feels funny. I'm beginning to enjoy these movements.

"Gradually sit up now and, as you do, move your arms around in front of you, behind you, to your right and left and even above you. If you touch someone say 'hello' but not with words, just with whatever part of your body is touching. Remember, you are learning where you are as an individual in space. The length of your arms and legs, your size and shape. This will be your home for many weeks, so come to know this space in which you now live. And, remember, no talking; for a while you must learn to express yourself with no words."

We stretched and stretched in all directions, first sitting and then standing. I began to like my place. The people in my group were strangers no longer. I was glad we were together, though my friends from my class were in other groups. I did not feel alone anymore.

"Now make your body as tall as you can. Stretch, come on, more, with your hands way, way up. Stretch as far over to the right as you can. Now to the left."

I felt I had doubled in size. When we went up, I must have been five feet tall at the tips of my fingers. Then she asked us to make our bodies just as small as we could. It was hard at first, but after many trials I found the right position. Funny, I was relaxed and not drowsy anymore. I was really coming to know my body—the soft places, the hard ones, what it could do being big and little, how it felt to touch and hold hands. I was not much aware of anything else or anyone else but me, my size, my shape, my skin, my muscles, even my bones.

"Now open your eyes and just stand quietly. How do you feel? I hope you're all feeling relaxed and ready to take a trip. In a few seconds I'd like you to lie down again and close your eyes. First I want to tell you something about breathing. Most often we just take little gulps of air and it passes quickly through our lungs and out our nose or mouth. But when you are tired, or tense, when you really want to relax you must learn to breathe deeply, all the way down in your abdomen, lower than your belly."

We were on our backs now and being told to take in a big gulp of air and to feel it down below our bellies—way down. We held the air and let it out slowly. Through our bodies it came, slowly all the way up and out through our mouths and noses. It felt like slow motion, so different because I was used to breathing quickly. But finally I caught on.

"Breathe deeply, way down, hold it, slowly let the air come up and out. Breathe again. Repeat."

It was now like a melody and it felt good. Over and over again, like the waves coming in and going out to sea. She was right, the air moved up from the abdomen, the stomach, the diaphragm, and lungs, and slowly out the mouth and nose. I was getting drowsy again. I could feel the rising and falling of other bodies around me, but mostly I was aware of my own. I was enjoying it. Then Dr. Perry's voice came back.

"Now you are ready to take a trip. In this trip you are to use your imagination, go someplace, either in this country or in another one or even to another planet. You can go alone or take someone with you. If you are alone, be aware of yourself in this place, notice your surroundings. If you are with someone, be aware of your feelings. Pay attention to your conversation. But mostly let your thoughts and feelings sail freely through you. Enjoy your trip."

It is quiet now. I can feel my breathing moving in and out. I can hear the breathing of others and the cars outside, and the sounds of the birds.

Dr. Perry's voice again: "It is important to empty your minds of all thoughts—like a blank sheet of paper on your desk. Fill it only with your trip."

It is silent again. Many ideas enter my mind—a magic forest filled with talking trees, a field of fairies dancing to the rhythm of the wind, floating on a soft cloud, the time I laughed till I was senseless at the circus, jumping off my rooftop, flying like an eagle. But none of these captured my attention for long. I remember now, something important, feeling deeply inside, the only time I've ever been to the seashore. When I entered the water, it was calm and I moved freely with my father. Then suddenly—where did it come from?—a strong, strong wind, huge waves coming into shore. We went out to meet them, twisting, turning, tumbling, with great glee and laughter. I can almost feel them now. The excitement of being lifted high up in the water and dropped sharply—again and again. Daddy, where are you now? Why don't we play like that any more?

And then, Dr. Perry's voice: "Take a few more minutes to bring your trip to a close."

Tears came down my face remembering that afternoon—the wind, the water, the movement. Dad catching me and holding me. I wish we had that feeling between us now.

Dr. Perry gave us time to talk about our trips and, with a little help, I shared mine. Most of the boys went on an adventure to the moon or to another planet, while the girls visited the zoo or told about a motor trip.

"Now that your bodies have been quiet such a long time we're going to wake them up. This will be a game like Simon Says. You watch me and when I do something, you do it, too. I hope you will relax the muscles of your body, use them freely, be aware of what happens as you exercise. Stand up. Put your arms at your sides. Remain silent a few minutes and breathe deeply. Now open your eyes.

"Simon says, tap the top of your heads. Harder. Put more life into it.

Simon says, tap your forehead, slowly, gently. Continue tapping in the same way, first gentle taps, then harder as you massage your eyes and all around your face."

This was fun. We tapped and slapped our necks and shoulders, up and down our arms, our chests, stomachs, thighs, legs, moved down the whole body and back up again. I wasn't sleepy anymore. I felt like running. So Dr. Perry said, "Go ahead, run in place, and notice how you're breathing."

Yes, it was a good feeling to be here, to feel relaxed and satisfied. I wish we didn't have to go back to our classrooms just yet, but I could see the hour was almost up.

"We have just about five more minutes and I know some of you want to move around. So I'll play one of my favorite records and you move around just in your own small groups at first. Then, as you feel the music, move freely anywhere in the room. Here goes Sammy Davis, Jr., singing 'I've Gotta Be Me.'"

I was surprised how quickly I began moving and how much fun it was to dance alone, to feel other bodies rushing past me, and most of all to know the feeling of being me.

Our special time ended, but we came back to this large room many times. At first we were learning to be aware of just ourselves, and to enjoy being alone. We learned what it means to be silently alone, to use no words. I learned to "talk" to myself only with feelings. I found out I was someone important. I felt it strongly with my group leader and with Dr. Perry. I knew how to breathe deeply and relax when I was in trouble and tense. I learned to enjoy my imagination. Exercising, playing, dancing, closing my eyes and feeling the life of my body, noticing my feelings—there were new experiences for me in school. I always came to these morning classes with a rush of joy and left slowly, feeling sad.

Each time we came we stayed in the same small group. After

we had a great many silent activities, we did a number of things using words and then shared them in our small groups.

"Today we're going to get into touch with a number of strong feelings that we all experience. As you sit there with your eyes closed, go to a time when you were feeling very angry. Create the scene in your own mind and try to recall how you felt, what you said, what happened. Talk silently to yourself and see what you can remember."

I get mad when anyone stops me from doing what I want to do or when someone calls me names like "stupid" or "dumb." Last year Mrs. Adams was always telling me how slowly I moved. She was always yelling at me. One day she said I must be stupid because I did everything in slow motion. I was angry. I felt like throwing a book at her but I didn't. She told me to take my seat, that I couldn't have recess. So I just pushed all my books on the floor. She came rushing at me, grabbed my arm, and we both looked ugly. She shoved me to a corner of the room and told me to stand there with my arms folded. Tears came down my face. I hated her. I never felt good ever in her class. I'm glad I'm with Mr. Swenson this year.

"Bring your angry scenes to a close now. Open your eyes and share your experience in your group. First show each person what your face and body look like when you are angry, then tell about it."

We each showed what it was like in our bodies to be angry. My eyes got big. My mouth shut tight and all my muscles strained. We each shared our anger with brothers, sisters, parents, teachers, friends. Then Dr. Perry spoke again.

"Some feelings we call negative feelings because they do not feel good. They upset us. Sometimes they leave us drained, worn out. Other feelings are called positive feelings. We enjoy them. We feel like dancing or singing or laughing and being silly. We feel good. Both the negative and positive feelings are important in being human. They help us to be alive. It's necessary to accept them, be honest with them. Don't run away from your negative feelings, face up to them. They'll help you to be a more exciting person and they'll help you enjoy your positive feelings even more.

"I would like you to close your eyes again and think of a time when you were very frightened. Remember what it was like, how you felt, what you said—not just the words but the feelings. Be aware of just what it is to be really scared."

The most frightened I've ever been was two weeks ago when Momma was very sick. She was in bed all day, sleeping, and Momma never is in bed during the daytime. I was scared she'd never wake up. I couldn't sleep. I had a bad dream and woke up. I thought she was dead. I lay in bed until daylight, then I went to see. I was really shaking when I opened her door and almost screamed when I saw that her bed was empty. Then I heard someone out in the kitchen and found her making breakfast. That was the happiest moment of my life.

"Everyone knows what it's like to feel hurt," Dr. Perry said. "Sometimes pain is physical and sometimes it's psychological. Today I want you to concentrate on what it feels like when someone you like says mean or nasty things to you, calls you names or hurts your feelings in other ways."

I feel bad whenever Momma yells at me or won't do something or take me somewhere. I feel hurt when my friends tease me. On the way to school yesterday Jay and Don were looking at some pictures in a magazine. I went up to them and they shut the book. They said they didn't want to walk to school with me, to go on ahead. I was with Jim so I didn't care about walking with them, but I was hurt they wouldn't let me see the pictures. I get along when I'm with one of them, but when they're together they always do something mean to me.

"This next feeling is a tricky one. Some people say it's a bad feeling and some say it's a good one. My own opinion is that it can be either, depending on what is happening. This feeling is called loneliness. You can be lonely when you're all alone and want someone to play with and there's no one around. You can be lonely when your Mom or Dad has punished you and sent you to your room and you lie on your bed or sit by yourself thinking that your Mom and Dad don't love you. Or, you can be lonely even when there are lots of people around, like in your classroom when people don't notice you, or ask your opinion, or invite you to play or when you feel very different in a bad way from anyone else—like when all the others are laughing at something that isn't funny to you or like when everyone else is enjoying the lesson and it doesn't make sense to you, or when all the others have the answers and you don't understand. All these feelings can be lonely feelings and you can feel sad, upset, small, unimportant.

"The other type of loneliness is when you really want to be alone to figure something out, to talk to yourself, to find out what you want to do. Or when you want to be alone with flowers or trees or watch a sunset or listen to voices of nature, the birds, the whispering leaves, the wind. Or sometimes when you've been around people too much and want to get off somewhere by yourself and just be with you. Choose one of these types of loneliness, the bad feeling of being alone, or the good feeling of being alone. Maybe you are feeling lonely right now. See if you can be aware, as you concentrate, of what it is really like to feel lonely."

My lonely times are all bad ones. Usually it's when someone doesn't want me around, when they tell me to get lost, my friends or my Dad. One time my brother cut me with a knife. My Momma was resting and said she didn't want to hear about it. I waited until Dad came home from work. He said he'd had a busy day and didn't want to be bothered. He turned on the television. There was no one to talk to. I felt miserable. I went and sat by myself and cried because no one cared that I was hurt. No one wanted to listen.

"Okay, enough of the heavy feelings. Let's all stand and shake every part of the body. First let's do the parts alone and then we'll do them all together. Start with your head. Shake. Shake. Now just your shoulders. Your arms. Okay, go ahead on your own. When you finish all the parts see how well you can shake your entire body. Hey, that's fine. Great! Now just let your arms dangle all the way down and breathe deeply—remember from all the way down and let the air come up slowly. Okay, everyone sit in your groups. There's too much noise in here. Wait a minute. From now on, when I raise my hand I want you all to raise your hands. That means stop talking, look in my direction, and listen.

"Let's go on with one of the most pleasant feelings—joy. Stop now, look into yourself. See if you can recapture a scene where your whole body tingled, where you laughed maybe until you cried. Close your eyes and concentrate."

The time I went to the circus we laughed and laughed at the clowns and the animal show. The funniest part was when all the clowns got out of a little car. They kept coming, more and more of them, and each time the one that came out was bigger. I enjoy coming here, too. I laughed a lot when you wanted us just to shake parts of our body. I thought it was silly. It was funny watching others. Joy is being silly, laughing, having a good time. I laugh when my Momma won't talk and all she'll do is make faces so I make faces back and we have fun playing this game.

"We only have time for one more of the positive feelings. This feeling is what makes being a person worthwhile. Some people believe that without it we'd all die. I won't tell you what it is, I'll show you. Denise, would you come up." Dr. Perry put her arms around Denise and held her close and hugged her. It didn't take long before we all yelled out LOVE! "Now take a journey to that moment when you were feeling love for someone and you felt love from that person. Be aware of what it is like when you are loving and being loved."

This one was easy. Every night Momma tells me a story before I go to sleep. We're all alone and she holds me close and lays down next to me. I feel warm and happy. I feel the whole world is beautiful and I'm glad I'm alive. My Momma feels warm and soft. We're together and I feel strong and at peace. I love my Momma and she loves me.

Our class was over, but we did not want to leave. Slowly we straggled out, holding on to the last moments. Dr. Perry added a word of encouragement, shouting, "I'll see you next week when we'll have lots of fun doing things with partners and pairs."

[clark moustakas]

SELF WITH ONE OTHER
Partners and Pairs

WE CONTINUED TO MEET in the large room week after week. One day Dr. Perry announced that we would no longer be alone, that it was time to make a switch. For many weeks to come we would be divided into partners or pairs.

"Stand up," she said, "just where you are, and stay in your small groups. First, let's all wake up. Shake your heads from side to side—gently. Now harder. Shake your arms and shoulders—one at a time. Both. Shake your right foot. Left foot. Now your whole body. Good. That was fun. Breathe deeply a few times.

"This morning we're going to work with partners. Stay in your own group and choose a partner." (Dr. Perry put her hand up— the sign to put our hands up and get quiet again.) "I'm going to show you how to learn to breathe with the same rhythm that your partner breathes. You must watch closely and pay attention so that you breathe just like your partner does. Barb, would you come up and be my partner? I'll try to match my breathing with yours. When you breathe in, I will, too. When you let the air out, so will I."

Dr. Perry took a few moments to see just how Barb was breathing, and then their two bodies moved up and down at the same time. It seemed silly but we all tried it. It looked easy but it wasn't. Jimmy and I had a hard time. We didn't like to look straight into one another's eyes, but it helped to watch closely. Dr. Perry came over and helped me find Jimmy's rhythm and we breathed in and out together. Then we changed and Jimmy found my rhythm and imitated it. This time the whole thing went much faster.

"Sometimes in school or at home we get the feeling that someone is pushing us into something or that we're being pulled without wanting to be. Keep your same partners and we'll try some pushing and pulling. Face each other, lock your fingers, and plant your feet on the floor, like this. Now one of you be the pusher and the other one let yourself be pushed."

Jimmy started pushing, and pushed me around the room. Then I pushed him. After that, we pulled each other. This was fun as we each had a chance to feel what it was like. Then Dr. Perry asked us to push together. Jimmy tried pushing me around but I stuck to my place and finally managed to push him back three or four feet. Some of us finished early and we sat down and started playing. Pretty soon we were making rowboats. Dr. Perry liked that and started singing "Row, Row, Row Your Boat." Everyone in the room was doing it now. We all sang and kept going back and forth until Dr. Perry interrupted us.

"Okay, I have something else to do. This time I would like you to change partners. Choose another person from your small group. One of you will be the leader and one the follower. After a while I'll ask you to change so each of you will have a turn to be leader. Put your hands up when you're ready to hear the instructions.

"I'm going to play some music, a record called *Joy*. I hope it will be fun for you. Wait a few moments until you really feel the music. Stay in place. Do not move around the room. Leaders move your arms and bodies and legs. Make different motions. Followers, your job is to make the same motions that your leaders are making, like in Simon Says. Okay, listen to the music and begin."

This was the most fun yet. Sheila was the leader first. She put her arms high in the air. So did I. Then she bent her body forward and backward. I followed. As the music got faster, Sheila moved fast but I kept up with her. Then I was the leader. I moved my legs up and down and Sheila kept up with me.

Dr. Perry interrupted. "This time, instead of continuing to move, when you find a position you like, stop. Freeze. Make a statue. Keep it for a while, then move on to other positions you like and make many different statues. Go ahead.

"That's wonderful. I really like the statues. Everyone sit down just where you are and rest a moment. This time we're going to do something tricky. I'll wait while you choose a new partner. Okay, I think everyone is ready. Milton, where's your partner? Oh, Fred —all right. For this one you either sit or stand, depending on what you decide to do. I'll demonstrate first. Who'll be my partner? Robin, Good! Okay, we'll call this Secret Messages. I will think of a message to send to Robin—without using any words, something like charades, if you've ever played that game. It's up to Robin to figure out and understand my message. She can talk but I can't. Nobody help Robin. Let her figure it out. You'll get your chance in a while."

Dr. Perry dribbled with her hand. Then she raised her body and tossed something into the air. Robin answered right away: "You like to play basketball." Then Robin did one and Dr. Perry got it.

I enjoyed sending secret messages with Shareda. Every time I see her in the hall now I send her a secret message and she answers me. We all do it in Mrs. Miller's class. When she tells us to stop talking and we want to say something, we do it with our eyes, our hands, and our bodies. I'm glad I learned how to use other ways when I want to talk with someone.

Dr. Perry's hand was up again. That was a silent message we all understood. So our hands went up and the room became quiet.

"We'll have time for just one more nonverbal person-to-person activity today. For this one, pair up with someone you haven't been with before. Good, I see that everyone has a partner. Before we get into this one, stay right where you are. Everyone knows how to breathe deeply. So do it until you establish a comfortable rhythm. Stay in place and breathe the way you would if you were sleeping.

Now, like you breathe when you first wake up. Walk around in a circle and notice what happens to your breathing. That's fine. This time run slowly in place. Run faster. Run in place as fast as you can. See how heavy your breathing becomes and how much it helps to breathe deeply. Okay, everyone sit down facing your partner and rest a while."

My last partner was Roger. Dr. Perry asked us to gently tap each other's head, face, shoulders, back, and legs. Then she suggested we slap a little harder. Roger was shy and didn't want to slap me, at first. Dr. Perry came over and stood next to us. Roger covered his face and wouldn't look at her. She told him if he didn't want to do it, it was okay. Then all of a sudden he looked at her, put his arms around me and started slapping my sides and back and legs. After a few moments I began slapping him, too. We were laughing hard together.

"Okay, everyone. Now that you are wide-awake it's time to go back to your classes. See if you can be aware of what's going on in you and around you today. Have a good day and keep your eyes and ears open."

I felt good leaving. I was beginning to feel free with my new friends—Jimmy, Sheila, Shareda, and Roger. None of them were in my class, but I see them in the hallways and in the lunchroom and sometimes during recess. I know how to relax. I know how to breathe. And, best of all, I know how to talk with my body when talking with my mouth is forbidden. Tuesday and Thursday mornings are my favorite days of the week. I can hardly wait for next Tuesday to come. I wonder what Dr. Perry will ask us to do then.

"I hope everyone had a good rest over the weekend. Are you ready to start? Take a few minutes, lay back, close your eyes, and just breathe quietly and relax for a while. Okay, everyone is quiet. I can hear your breathing. Today we'll be using words—so let's all be silent for a few more minutes and listen. I like the way Jimmy is breathing. He seems to be completely relaxed.

"All right, our first activity requires that you listen carefully to me. Think about a day in school. Your teacher, Mrs. King, has written some words on the board and asks you to copy them. You know that later she will ask you to read them. You start but are having trouble with some of the words. Mrs. King tells you to stand up and read. Stop dawdling, she says. What's the matter with you? Remember how you felt, what you wanted to do, what it was like. Okay, concentrate on that scene."

I always had trouble with Mrs. Bailey. She was never satisfied with anything I did, so when she turned her back to write on the board, I always messed up—pushing and teasing people around me. Sometimes I looked out the window and watched cars go by and saw what kind they were, but mostly I dreamed about things I wanted to do and thought about what was going to happen when I got home. Dr. Perry asked us to choose a partner and tell how we felt when a teacher yelled at us or put us down. I chose Bill and told him about Mrs. Bailey.

"This time take a moment and notice each person in your group. Choose someone you have a problem with. Think for a while. How do you feel when that person is bothering you. Now in a quiet voice tell that person what he does to annoy or irritate you."

Sheila is sometimes a pest. I don't like it when she starts pushing and shoving me and telling me what to do. She's too bossy. So I chose Sheila as my partner and told her but she didn't say anything. She listened and then just giggled.

"Okay, stand up, everybody. Let your bodies relax and expand, stretch all your muscles, let your arms dangle freely—like this. Now tighten every muscle as tight as you can and stretch them as high as you can. When you can't tighten anymore or stretch anymore, yell as loudly as you can—just once—and let your whole body relax again."

I never heard so much yelling in school. I guess Dr. Perry knows what she's doing. It is fun. I wonder what's going to happen now.

"Okay, everyone sit down. This time imagine you are all alone. You don't have any friends. Look at each person in your small group. Choose someone you'd like to be your friend. Think about yourself. Take a few minutes and think about all the things you enjoy doing. Then tell the person you choose that you want to be friends. Tell the person all you can about yourself that will help the other person to decide whether he wants you as a friend. Think it over before you begin. Then choose someone and go ahead."

I've liked Jimmy since we first came into the big room, but most of the time he's with boys from his own class. I said: "Jimmy I want to be your friend and play with you after school. I like baseball and basketball and I like to go to movies. If you come to my house, we can play and watch television or we can go sledding." We put our arms around each other and Jimmy said he'd come to my house after school.

Dr. Perry played a record and we all ran around and danced in the room. Then we went back to our classrooms. Jimmy and I walked out together. I have a new friend and won't have to wait until Thursday to see him again.

The large group meetings emphasizing communication, relationships, and sharing in partners and pairs continued over a period of three months. At the end of this time we met in separate classrooms and continued to create partner-and-pair activities. The aim of these activities was to foster in-depth relations, especially to reach withdrawn, isolated, friendless children. A number of examples are presented below, the first by Karen Shelley.

[karen shelley]

While Mrs. Freeman's second-grade class was busy with reading workbooks, I asked three children to join me in the hall for a discussion of friendship. Donald, Reginald, and Geraldine were chosen from among the volunteers.

These children talked for ten minutes about why they like to have friends, what they like to do with their friends, and how it feels to move to a new school and make new friends. Donald and Geraldine talked frequently during this discussion. Reginald, who is *very* quiet in class and often seems fearful, said little—but he did answer a few questions and seemed happy to be involved in the experience.

I asked the children if they had a special friend in their class and if they played with this friend outside of school. Reginald lives several blocks away and said that he doesn't see his classmates after school. Then I asked them if there was someone in the class that they would like for a friend. They all named someone. I asked them if they would like to go back into the room and invite these children to join our group. They were excited about doing this.

When the other three children were brought out, we shared with them the discussion that had led up to their joining us. I then asked them if they would like to spend some time alone with their partners to get to know one another better and share their feelings about friendship.

Reginald was very shy in the beginning and his friend, Terry, did a lot of giggling, but after they were left alone for a while (the other two pairs were immediately involved in the experience), they began to talk together. I couldn't hear what they were saying, but they later told me that they were planning to visit each other and were trying to explain the directions for getting to their homes.

I heard part of the girls' discussion. Geraldine asked Doris, "If I come to your house, will you come out and play with me?" Doris said that she wouldn't because she was afraid to go out of her house. At this point, Geraldine turned to me. She said she couldn't understand that reply. I suggested they might talk about it some more. Then Doris told Geraldine why she was afraid. Some members of her family had had some frightening experiences in the neighborhood, so she rarely left her home without an adult.

Donald and Marvin began talking about things they like to do with friends. Donald said he likes to go to the store with his friend to buy candy that they can share. Marvin said he likes to have friends because they can play with each other, especially baseball and football. Donald replied that he was going to bring a football to school so they could play with all their friends. Donald and Marvin then talked about their experiences with boats and with hunting. Donald said that "rabbits taste nasty." At this, Marvin jumped up and, in a spirit of fun, said, "Boy, I could bop you in the mouth for that." He then went on to tell Donald how his grandfather hunted rabbits. During the last few minutes, they talked about dreams that they had had about each other. These "dreams" were adventure stories that always included the two of them, and they excitedly took turns telling them to each other.

The sharing time lasted about fifteen or twenty minutes. All of the children became increasingly animated. There was movement and warm physical contact. They seemed to be enjoying one another thoroughly. I can't express to you in words the joy that I felt coming from the children during this experience.

We came together again before returning to the room. The children spent a few minutes sharing within our small group. I then asked them if they would like to tell the rest of the class about our experience. They were eager to do so.

Meanwhile, back in the classroom, there was much curiosity about what was happening in the hall. When we returned, the class wanted to hear the children talk about their experience. We then repeated the process with the entire class.

After most of the class had chosen their partners, there were four or five children still moving around the room. One little girl, Maria, was crying. When I asked her why she was crying, she replied that nobody wanted to be her friend. I told her that I wanted to be her friend and asked if she would like to talk with me. She said that she would.

When we were alone, she told me that Lucille didn't want to be her friend. Apparently she had then asked Frankie to be her partner and was also turned down. (Lucille is a little girl who seems to work hard at alienating others.) I asked Maria if she wanted Lucille to be her friend. She didn't answer. I asked her if she liked Lucille. No answer. Maria stopped crying and seemed to be feeling much better. (My interpretation of this is that Maria had not been thinking about her own feelings toward Lucille, but only of Lucille's rejection of her.)

[nancy boxill]

With my first-grade group, I started off talking about how it would feel to have a place of your own. We talked about why you would want a place of your own and the kinds of things you could do with such a place. Then I read a story, "Evan's Corner," about a little boy who wanted a place of his own and what he did with it. I then asked the children to choose a partner and share with them their thoughts on where their place would be and what they would do with it.

Barbara and Jane

> *Barbara.* I'm goin' to a playground and get me some plants and water them and put them in a window; den I'm gonna paint me something and put it on my wall.
>
> *Jane.* Where you gonna be sitting?
>
> *Barbara.* Nobody gonna touch me 'cause I be lonely, nobody gonna mess with me. Den I goin' to the grocery store and get me some orange crates and den my mother gonna come say "You still lonely?" and I'm gonna say "Yes, mama."

Jeff and Willie

> *Jeff.* I gonna go upstairs and den make me a house wit wood and I'm gonna make me a bed and I'll bring all my toys in it, that's all.
>
> *Willie.* I found me a house, den I go to the corner, buy me some newspaper, den I buy me a set, den I go and get some furniture, den I buy me some ice cream and some juice and den I go downtown and buy me a coat.

[marilyn malkin]

For the discussion in pairs in Mrs. Henderson's class (second grade), we used the topic Friendship. To begin, the whole class came together as a group and we talked about what it means to be a friend and to have a friend, what kinds of things friends do with and for each other, and what it feels like not to have any friends. Then I read them two short stories dealing with friendship. The first was "May I Bring a Friend?" by Beatrice Schenk de Regniers, and the second was "Let's Be Enemies" by J. M. Udry. We talked about friendship a little more and I showed them pictures of children who might be friends. At this point the children picked partners to discuss friendship. I didn't get anything down verbatim except for phrases like "We be friends," and "Sometimes I share ma washin machine wi' ma frien." They were just talking too fast and I didn't feel that I could stay with one group the whole time. They were talking with each other of very concrete experiences with friends and when we came together again to finish off, they related some of these.

I felt that they enjoyed the time talking to just one other person. One pair I noticed took turns relating incidents to each other, and each of them really listened to what the other person had to say. I was pleased with the way the whole thing worked, especially since this was the first time we had tried it. I think that this is something which we should repeat to give the children practice in relating to just one other person.

[suzanne toaspern]

This project was about friendship. First we all sat down in one large group (the entire first grade together). I asked the children to pick a partner—I told them that they would be talking with this person in a little while. Most people found a partner right away—but there were a few people who didn't. Several children wanted to be with the same other child. We talked about it a while and I asked a few people to be together who hadn't picked each other. They said Okay, but later these few people had a hard time talking with their partners and seemed very shy.

We talked as a large group about friendship. I began by reading them parts of a book we had read together before—*The Bigger They Come*. We talked some about what it was like to be new and have no friends, and why the boy in the book wanted friends, and how he felt when he danced to the music of friendship. Then I showed the children some pictures of friends that I got at the Detroit Public Library Schools Department. We talked about all the different people who could be our friends and the children told of different experiences they had had with friends.

Then I asked the children to sit down somewhere with their partner. I asked them to think of a friend in their minds. Do you have a friend you are thinking of? Yes. Okay then, tell your partner about your friend and then listen while he tells you about his friend. Most everyone began eagerly to talk. Some of the children put their faces very close together and talked intently. I think generally the children really enjoyed this chance to listen and talk. I think it is often hard for them to wait their turn when we talk as a big group.

The children talked very concretely about their friends. They told about things they had done with their friends—how they would go over to their friends' houses and play with their friends. One boy told about the fight he had had with his friend and how afterward they were still friends. Another boy told about how he and his friend had been playing with their "big wheels" and he had fallen off his and bumped into a wall.

It was hard for me to write down specifically what they were saying. When I got close enough to hear, they would include me in the conversation. Generally, though, it seemed that they talked in running narratives. For example: "We went over to Keith's house an' then we was riding our bikes an' then we was at the store, we bought some candy, an' then Eric came over, he was chasing us . . ."

[carolyn veresh]

This morning I wanted to explore experiences the children had had when they felt unloved and unwanted. I was interested in how one child relates such times to one other child. Each child would be paired with another he had chosen and with whom he felt comfortable working for a morning of activities. I had planned three activities I thought would help the children to share their experiences and emotions with their partner. First, each pair would participate in some nonverbal experiential exercises; next, each pair would be listening to a story; and finally, I would ask each pair to find a spot away from the others so that they could talk between themselves.

For the next thirty to forty minutes we shared several nonverbal experiential exercises designed specifically for pairs. We began with breathing exercises, each child feeling with his hands the other's chest and listening with his ears to their partner's deep breathing. We moved through foot-washing, rocking—in the form of "Row, Row, Row Your Boat"—exploring each other's space, back-rubbing, and push-pulling, and we ended with deep breathing. This nonverbal time of beginning to know and experience one another, I was hoping, would help them to loosen and free some hesitations they may have had in sharing innermost fears.

Keeping in mind the pairing, I asked each pair to come, hand in hand, over to the story area. The story I had chosen was to help stimulate their thoughts and feelings about times when they had felt unloved and unwanted. The story was from the DUSO kit and was entitled "You Don't Love Me Anymore." The story is about a little girl named Mary Ann who is punished and sent to her room by her mother. When Mrs. Johnson asks Mary Ann if she knows why she was punished, Mary Ann replies that it was because her mother doesn't love her anymore. To illustrate that parents punish because they do love children, Mrs. Johnson recalls how they punished their dog, Wags, when he chased cars because they didn't want Wags to get hurt. The story talked of the feelings of imagining you are unloved. I encouraged them to talk of the times they had felt unloved. We also talked about how it feels to feel loved, to be kind, to be unkind, to cry, to hate, to be punished, to feel sorry for something you did, and to forgive.

The pairs had had two different experiences, the nonverbal exercises and listening to the story. Now we would bring the morning's activities to a close with each pair finding a spot away from the other pairs and talking and sharing with each other a time they had felt unloved and how that experience felt in terms of inside emotions— sad, hateful, sorry, angry, unfairly treated, rejected, and so on. Following are some of the dialogues different pairs shared with each other.

"One time I was playing on the playground and my daddy come and got me and punished me—he beat on me and I was really afraid and scared and he made me stay in my room and I felt really bad."

"My sister is always beating on me and picking on me, and she wakes me up and fights with me—she's always picking on me —and one of my cousins was fighting with me and I got really mad and scratched him—see, just like this—and blood ran all down his face and I was really scared and we kept on fighting."

"We always go to church every Sunday, and one time my auntie was home alone and my dogs, Salty and Pepper, were there, too, and this man broke into my house and stole my auntie's radio, color TV, money, and killed my dogs and stole some of my money. I felt really sad and I cried and cried."

"You shouldn't tease people, because it makes them feel sad and cry. I don't like it when you do that to me. It makes me cry."

[clark moustakas]

ENCOUNTERS IN LEARNING

For TWO WEEKS I REMAINED a silent observer in a second-grade classroom as children moved in a uniform way and followed instructions in a schedule that repeated itself daily. It was evident from the first day that teaching was a continual effort but that learning was minimal. During the reading assignments children could identify most of the words, but I soon learned that many of them could recognize the words only in the context in which they were used, and often only when pictures were included. They often did not know what the words actually meant; they were completely lost when a word had multiple meanings or when illustrations were eliminated.

The rebels in this second-grade classroom were a group of boys who somehow always managed to impede Mrs. Young's instructions; they interfered by using rumbling and other tactics when her back was turned and by being awkward and obtuse when they met her face to face. The louder Mrs. Young shouted her instructions, the higher the noise level became. I rarely have seen children move more quickly to get what they wanted, as soon as she began writing on the blackboard or turned her back. Nor have I witnessed such a degree of slow-motion behavior when Mrs. Young was "teaching" and urging children to pay attention. Finally, in desperation, she would start shoving chairs around, screaming, threatening, and sometimes hitting. When this happened, for a brief time there was a frozen silence. The children were like privates facing their general, but even after a third or fourth repetition of the assignment, I could see as I moved around the room that scarcely half knew what they were doing. Most children were copying the words off the board, but at the same time they appeared to be in a trancelike, dreamy state, in another world. As long as they were quiet, Mrs. Young usually left them alone.

My task in joining the group was to find a way of introducing human values, of encouraging freedom, involvement, and responsibility in learning. I was looking for an opening to begin my own work during these first two weeks, but the drills within activities and the shift from one activity to the next were so rapid that I saw no place to enter.

One child especially intrigued me—Anthony. He was Mrs. Young's Public School Enemy #1. During one hour, I counted fifteen times when she verbally attacked him: "Dumb," "Stupid," "Troublemaker," "Misfit," and other such insults were used. He answered back with his body, and particularly with his eyes. They had a running feud which almost daily ended in physical punishment and disaster. Usually Anthony got his licks in, aggravating, frustrating, and humiliating Mrs. Young, slowing up her schedule, and often so demoralizing her that she would sit down in exhaustion, sigh heavily, and breathe deeply for several minutes. She told me that she was sure he was mentally retarded and heading for juvenile delinquency. Without success, she had tried to transfer him to a special classroom. Anthony was the leader of a gang of five boys, and when he was in trouble the others saw it as their duty to go into action, undermining in devious ways whatever Mrs. Young was trying to do. The climax was reached one day during a reading assignment. The "fast" group was in the back of the room with Mrs. Young, while the slow readers were being helped by Miss Baylor, the paraprofessional who assisted every morning. Anthony, by the second week of my visit, was sending me frequent nonverbal messages. On this day he signaled that Mrs. Young was on the warpath and was out to get him. She kept him fastened to her all morning, and though he was a "very slow reader" at this point he was in the middle of the fast group. As she turned to instruct a child on how to read orally, Anthony moved his chair away. She grabbed him and pulled him back, holding his arms tightly. This was repeated many times; each time he was pulled back he managed to increase the momentum of the pull, thus crushing his chair against her. Though she winced when Anthony hit his target, she did not utter a word. After four crashes her anger reached a peak and she slapped him across the face. He retaliated by shoving onto the floor the reading books of as many children as he could reach. Mrs. Young slapped him again. He tipped his chair over against her, ending up on his back on the floor but not before he managed to kick her effectively. At this point, Mrs. Young threw up her arms and shouted to me, "Okay, Dr. Clark, Anthony is your boy for the rest of the morning. See what you can do with him. I give up. He's hopeless."

I suggested to Anthony that we return to his own seat. He followed me to his place:

"Anthony, we have the rest of the morning for you to do anything you wish. Is there something now you feel like doing?" Anthony stared at me for a long time, nodded affirmatively, and proceeded to the classroom cupboard. He brought back a huge mound of clay and immediately went to work, forming and shaping what appeared to be a high wall or fence. Then he began making a variety of animals and placed them inside. Gradually, his five friends formed a circle around him, and as they watched they understood what he was creating and began to help. At one point, Isaac wanted to make a giraffe and asked Anthony to help him. Without a word, Anthony pulled out his reading text, immediately found the picture and showed it to Isaac. The group worked together in almost complete silence until they finished the project.

"Anthony, I think there's a story behind that wall and all those animals. If you want to tell it to me, I'll write it down."

Before Anthony could respond, Mrs. Young screamed, "What

are all you boys doing over there? Dr. Clark, they're supposed to be reading. This isn't play time."

"Okay, Mrs. Young," I answered. "We're just heading toward reading. Go ahead with your story, Anthony."

"This here is a high, high fence. All these little animals are inside and they can never get away. They are hungry. They want something to eat. She is the zoo master and she's big and mean. She only gives them scraps for food. They are so hungry, they are weak and they are dying. One day the zoo master notices them. She sees how skinny they are and how slowly they move. She feels sorry for them. She gathers all the food she can find and opens the gate. The animals come out and eat and eat and eat. But, it is too late, and they all die. The zoo master is sorry she waited so long."

"Anthony, would you like to make a large mural to cover the board and we can put your story on it?" In unison, the boys shouted affirmatively. From the roll of paper, I took about ten feet as Mrs. Young, with widening eyes, watched it unfurl.

"Dr. Clark, what are you doing with all that paper?" she asked in a sharp tone.

"We're putting Anthony's story on it and maybe he can read it to the class then."

Silently, skeptically, she went on with her reading group. As I rewrote the story, Anthony and his friends drew with crayons around the letters and spaces, reproducing the fence and figures of the clay sculpture. With masking tape we put the mural on the blackboards. The front wall of the room was almost fully covered.

I asked Anthony if he would read it to the entire class. With great excitement, he procured the pointer and was ready to begin. I suggested we practice first and he agreed. With help from his friends and from me, to my surprise he could read the story, recognizing many of the words himself. Anthony seemed to grow a foot taller as he and his group read the story. Mrs. Young was genuinely impressed and led the applause. "Okay, Dr. Clark," she said, "from now on those six boys are yours when you come." The children shouted joyously, surrounded me, and we threw our arms around one another. Anthony had found a way to be, and he left for lunch wide-eyed and happy.

From that week, Barb, my colleague and graduate student from Merrill-Palmer, and I worked together in creating projects that would bring a new spirit and life into the classroom. As Mrs. Young saw the responses of the children, she began joining us; sometimes she suggested activities herself. Miss Baylor also caught the spirit of our efforts and became an essential person in many of the projects. We discovered that if we could integrate music, art, literature, dramatics, and movement into the learning experiences of Anthony's second-grade classroom, we consistently got a strong response from the children. They became intensely interested, involved, committed to stretching themselves, expressing their potentials and abilities. We tapped into the type of situation that would bring excitement and vitality into the learning process. Often we used a multimedia approach. We used rock music as background for finger painting and storytelling; constant favorites were The Supremes, The Jackson Five, and The Temptations. Interspersed with painting and drawing, the children, individually and as a group, created live movements and rhythms. In one project the children wrote stories on the back of their paintings. This was followed by a practice session in pairs and triads. They read their stories to one another until they could recognize the words. Often they corrected the spelling. Sometimes the stories were read aloud to the entire group.

Another project involved writing poetry. We used Richard Lewis' collections of children's poems—especially *Miracles*—the Japanese collection *There Are Two Lives,* and the Eskimo poems *I Breathe A New Song.* With a musical background and the opportunity to draw freely, the children created their own poems with eagerness and involvement. Sometimes we asked them to dramatize their poems and stories. The drama could be nonverbal, in pantomime or a kind of movement or dance that would create the feeling of letters or words. Sometimes they developed elaborate skits to recapture the message in the painted scenes.

Another resource that was effective in arousing and sustaining interest and involvement in learning was the use of tape recordings and videotaping in the form of dramatics, "radio" interviewing, and talent shows. We had one session on "feeling-words," in which each child wrote on colored slips of paper the words he used to express different feelings. We ended up with about sixty different words, which were then put on the blackboard. Each child who wanted to, read the words that fitted his experience, and made up a story with them. Several discussions followed in which children shared personal experiences. We developed a number of dance stories that depicted major emotional experiences—anger, fear, joy, love, loneliness, sorrow, pain, and hatred. Children then danced these feelings and put them into stories. Sometimes the children worked best alone, sometimes in pairs or triads, and sometimes in small groups. Occasionally the entire class worked together, but only rarely was this the preferred way. We tried to discover the most effective structuring from the activity itself, the moods of the children, and their immediate preferences.

The four adults also eventually learned to work well together and Mrs. Young came to value the free, human ways of bringing zest and life to the learning situation. She herself was more comfortable with a balance of traditional assignments and spontaneous use of art, music, drama, and movement. The climate of learning changed radically. Mrs. Young and Anthony became friends. Her description of him to others in the school differed markedly from what it had been at the beginning of the year. Their feud ended with the zoo story. Their relationship came to be rooted in positive values, the most distinctive of which were feelings of mutual respect and acceptance. They were not only able to work together but could also joke and have fun, and they could get angry without resorting to hostile tactics. They were now obviously comfortable with one another, in contrast to their mutual wary vigilance and vengeance of the first few months.

Roger and I both felt the teacher's angry expression as we entered the classroom, but the cold reception dissipated when we met the children's sparkling eyes. The nonverbal communication we had tried hard to develop was clearly at work. The children let us know that we were welcome. Several of them motioned to vacant chairs and invited us to sit down. They continued sending us messages and with their eyes and bodies communicated their joy. The first few weeks in this classroom were tense ones. Mrs. Allen obviously was threatened by our presence. Several times she just glared at us, especially when we came into the room. Although she had volunteered to participate in our project, she was upset and disturbed. We later learned that the visual communication that we had interpreted as anger was really a look of frustration and bewilderment. "What did we intend doing? How did we want her to participate?"

In the early visits we moved around the room assisting children with the assignments. In reading, Mrs. Allen was using the Sullivan programmed word series. We learned that although most children could identify the words correctly when pictures were associated with them, covering up the pictures almost always resulted in failure. Further, common words that had different meanings in different contexts were puzzles for even the "fastest" readers. For example, "tug" always meant tugboat, rather than pull or toil or drag or even tow. The word could not be identified by many children when the picture was covered up. We reached the same kind of conclusion with arithmetic assignments. In spite of modern methods, these first graders were memorizing and learning fixed or rigid facts rather than concepts and principles. Changing the context of numbers almost always resulted in confusion and failure.

Since our primary purpose in being in the classroom was to introduce creative and artistic processes into learning—to see ways of including art materials, music, dramatics, and rhythms—we asked Mrs. Allen for a conference to discuss concrete ways in which we could become involved. Even more important was the clearing up of misunderstandings between us. I confronted her with my feeling that she resented our coming to her classroom. To my surprise, she denied any resentful feelings and indicated that her facial expressions were those of bewilderment. She wanted to help but was baffled. She also stated that she knew her teaching was too rigid and that staying with traditional methods was not satisfying. Our presence made her feel even more inadequate. The idea of open communication threatened her, but she was willing to work on it. Since children rarely approached her on a personal level, she was unsure of how they really felt about her. An important outcome of the conference was her stated desire to modify her teaching methods and her willingness to work with us. Because of her anxiety in open-ended learning, she requested that we bring a tentative outline of what we hoped to do and that we take a few minutes before each session to consult with her.

In time, Mrs. Allen and Mrs. Munson, the paraprofessional, contributed significantly to bringing more life into the classroom. They brought projects of their own that grew out of children's feelings and interests. The lively expressions of the children could readily be seen once our work got under way.

To break completely away from the usual setup, for most sessions we moved all the tables and chairs against the wall and used the floor space—which fortunately was carpeted. This class met in a portable building, due to overcrowded conditions in the main building of the school, but this was advantageous in many ways, since we didn't have to be concerned about the noise level.

Our first approach utilized imagination, storytelling, and dramatization. In the beginning, the children felt comfortable only with stories that were very familiar. We divided the class into four small groups, with one adult joining each group. In each group a story was read and the group was given time to work out a dramatization of it. The skit was then performed before the entire class. Sometimes we used background music. At other times we asked the children to draw some scene in the story that they especially liked or disliked. In time, some of the children learned to create their own stories, to improvise and to use pantomime and other nonverbal ways of conveying messages. They definitely gained more poise and confidence. Children who were shy or withdrawn in the early weeks became more outgoing in approaching others and more responsive in communication. One day stands out particularly. We decided to dramatize classroom scenes. The children found this especially difficult. Even when they had worked out a play in advance they were unable to perform it. As we discussed the problem, it became clear that they were afraid of hurting Mrs. Allen's feelings and afraid, too, of what she might do. Mrs. Allen herself opened the issue, stating that she knew they were afraid of her. It was an exciting exchange in which barriers on both sides came down. An open, free discussion took place and the morning culminated in the creation of scenes that mimicked Mrs. Allen's tone of voice, her facial expressions, her methods of handling problem situations, and her teaching approach. It was a real breakthrough. From that day on, a more open and spontaneous communication developed between Mrs. Allen and the children.

From dramatics, we moved to a concentration on activities that facilitated the expression and sharing of dreams, nightmares, fears, anger, and love. Our general approach was to use all the space, encouraging each child to find his spot, to work alone and later share with others, either in small groups or in the total group. Often we started with a story or discussion that provided background for the experience. We then asked the children to draw their feelings and recreate the scene or convey the nature of the experience. Often we used musical themes as background music; for example, in the "dreams and nightmares" project we used the space music from the film 2001. Sometimes the adults served as guides in helping individual children; sometimes they created drawings and stories, too. The sharing sessions took many forms: small group discussions, radio interviews, total group interchange. Often individual children requested special time with one of the adults to discuss the experience. Sometimes we ended our sessions with rhythms and dancing, usually to rock music.

The children shouted with joy as we entered the room. Mrs. Allen came to value these mornings also, but she still preferred a clear demarcation between Merrill-Palmer mornings and other mornings. When we were present she often became a person, but on other days she remained, on the whole, a teacher and sought to stay within the traditional confines of the curriculum. Occasionally, however, she would share with us her excitement in suddenly doing a creative program with the children on her own.

Our most ambitious project occurred during the last three months of the school year. Each child agreed to make a book. We cut out papers and stapled them together and each person made a cover design. We were enthralled by the variety and uniqueness of each design. The individuality of each child was clearly present in color, shape, form, content—in contrast to our first several meetings, in which the work of a few served as models for the entire group. At that time it was Mrs. Allen who spoke out against the uniformity. It was she who insisted that the children find their own space in the room apart from others and work alone. This separation, each child having his own special space in which to work, proved to be an important factor in nurturing the individuality that increasingly developed.

Many different types of experiences went into the book. Our approach continued to include the use of music, art, literature, drama, and movement. Now we also wanted to focus on the senses of touch, taste, smell, vision, and sound, and on extrasensory experiences. Each project became a page or chapter in the book.

We started by asking each child to write on large colored rectangles his favorite words. Once again, the variety impressed us— Love, Spring, Record Player, Easter, Christmas, Fun, Momma, Daddy, and many other words appeared, none of them from their Sullivan list. The children printed or wrote the words with a great deal of excitement, helped one another spell them, read them to one another, read them to the four adults. Then they pasted them onto large sheets of paper and inserted them in their books. The children used these words and others in writing "Get Well" cards to one of the adults who was in the hospital following an auto accident. Each card was a unique expression of the child and contained his own special words. Eventually the cards also went into the books.

One day we decided to explore the immediate neighborhood. We divided the children into four groups, each group traveling its own way. The task was to observe anything of interest and on returning to make a drawing and label the scene. The trip itself was an opportunity to share neighborhood and family activities and experiences, to develop relationships with other children and the adult leader, and to notice and really become aware of the neighborhood itself. Part of the trip was made in silence in order to accent the visual experience. Upon returning, the children drew scenes and used captions to depict what had affected them most. Again, language was part of the experience, and spelling and word recognition became important. With great joy the children created their scenes and shared them—clouds, broken windows, lines on the pavement, damaged autos, short scruffy grass, trees, dogs and cats, dilapidated steps, dust and smoke, people walking silently, people quarreling, flowers, paper-littered streets, cans and broken bottles, a lost mitten. These pictures and stories also went into their books.

Experiences of loneliness were discussed after a reading of *Crow Boy* by Yashima. The children, almost without exception, identified with Chibi. Most had stories to tell, some of these relating to classroom experiences of feeling alone and without any friends. We played, softly, music from *The Lion in Winter* and the children drew "I Am Lonely" scenes. These involved feelings following illness, feelings of being rejected, being put down and feeling small, being unfairly punished, being home alone, having no one to play with, feeling left out, hearing parents and other adults fighting.

One day we emphasized the importance of listening, discussing how much we miss by not really hearing what goes on around us. Again we decided to tour the neighborhood in small groups, remaining absolutely silent and listening for different sounds. Each group went off in a different direction. The walk lasted about half an hour and when we returned we asked the children to draw pictures of each sound, and where the sound came from. We asked them to label each picture with the sound itself. This again was a joyous activity; the entire room was alive, each child creating his sounds in a cartoonlike fashion. The adults moved around the room and helped only when requested. The outcome was an ingenious collection of sounds, among them: VROOM—a car rushing by; SCREECH—breaks squealing; SH-SH-SH—windshield wipers moving back and forth; WHEEE—sounds of sirens; OOFF, OOFF—a dog barking; CHIRP-CHIRP-CHIRP—birds singing; YOW-YOW-YOW—a mother screaming at her child; CLICK-CLICK—footsteps on the walk; ONG-ONG—groaning of a steam shovel; SSSS—the fluttering of leaves; WHOO-WHOO—the blowing wind. This experience was shared in pairs and in small groups. The pictures were added to the books.

We brought in many different kinds and colors of fabrics for children to touch, feel, explore. Each child chose those that looked and felt good and created designs and pictures. The fabrics were used in a variety of art projects with particular emphasis on touch, warmth, nearness, distance, detachment. Again new words were learned and used.

Mrs. Allen and her assistant, Mrs. Munson, became integral people in the projects. On many occasions when Roger and I were not present they introduced activities of their own. A free, spontaneous communication developed among us. The cooperative spirit we shared was clearly reflected in the children's relaxed and expressive behavior. This was another contrast to the early weeks.

On many occasions we danced together and could let go freely in movement. This was one activity to which nearly every child consistently responded with enthusiasm and asked for more. Often the movement sessions started with individuals moving alone to the music. In a natural way the individual expressions shifted to pairs, then small groups, and almost every dance session ended with the entire group moving together. Rock music was by far the favorite kind of music used.

One final book project involved the use of smell. For this we again toured the neighborhood around the school. We structured the experience to include only growing things. During the walk-around the children at first ran from one small plot of grass to another, exclaiming in surprise that each blade of grass had a different smell, and that each plot of grass had a common odor that was different from other plots. They smelled leaves from different trees and from the same trees, flowers from the same clump and from different ones, flowering shrubs in different stages of development, wild plants of various kinds. Without exception, the children became aware of the uniqueness of smell for each flower though it was of the same kind as the others around it; they learned that each living thing has a distinct odor. Soon they could identify from a distance which growing things gave off an odor, which were pungent or fragrant, and which had a definite stench. They could identify also the connection between smell and taste as we gave them samples of spices, herbs, and other seasonings—sweet, bitter, sour, tangy, or salty. Drawings of smell and taste were made and labeled. These, too, were added to their books.

At the end of the year each child had an opportunity to share his book. It was amazing how consistently the children could identify their favorite words, though many of these were far beyond first-grade level. Not just words, however, but feeling experiences, aesthetic experiences, and the life of the senses were part of their learning and living. Each book was a unique expression of the person who created it. And each child went off with it proudly, a real accomplishment to share with parents and other interested adults. There were no evaluations, no grades, no ranking. In this project every person stood out in confidence, in self-esteem, in the sense of having worked and played in making worthy creations.

[cereta perry]

As we worked in the classrooms, we were constantly seeking ways to develop activities that would help primary children get more fully involved in the process of self-understanding. One result of my search was the discovery of DUSO, a program of activities designed to be used by regular classroom teachers of primary classes.[1] The program is based on the conviction that teachers can be effective agents in helping children meet the normal developmental problems confronting them as they learn to become effective persons.

I introduced DUSO, the blue-and-white dolphin, to a primary II class of children, explaining that DUSO was willing and eager to help them develop an understanding of themselves, their classmates, their teachers, and their parents. I then showed them the other puppets who would assist DUSO in the exciting task of understanding self and others. The helpers included an adult male, an adult female, two male children, and two female children. As these puppets were passed around, the children experienced great fun in

[1] Don Dinkmeyer, "DUSO Kit D-1" (Circle Pines, Minnesota: American Guidance Services, Inc.). DUSO: Developing understanding of self and others.

handling them and in giving them names. In addition to the puppets, other materials in the DUSO program are:

a manual: A clear, concise guide for teachers containing suggestions for administering the many activities included.

two storybooks: Collections of interesting and stimulating stories that deal with normal developmental problems which children encounter.

posters: Thirty-three color posters, 15″ x 19″, each of which presents the main point in one of the stories.

cassettes: Cassettes containing forty-one songs which accompany the stories and the supplementary activities.

puppetry and role-playing cards: Thirty-three cards providing instructions for supplementary activities involving the children in real-life situations.

puppet props: Play props, in color, scaled to allow children to create appropriate settings for their activities.

The children were given opportunities to get acquainted with the materials that interested them most. Following this period of exploration, they listened to a song and learned to sing it with joy and gusto. It became the practice to launch each DUSO session with:

Hey DUSO, come on out,
Hey DUSO, come on out,
We like to listen and talk with you,
We like your songs and stories too,
Hey DUSO, come on out.

Following the invitation to DUSO to come out, "The Red and White Bluebird" was the first story to be introduced. The story is part of the unit entitled "Understanding and Accepting Self." After the children heard the story, they became involved in a discussion of what they liked about themselves. At the close of the discussion the children joined in singing:

So long, DUSO, see you again,
So long, DUSO, see you again,
It's good to know that you are there

To talk with children everywhere.

So long, DUSO, see you again.

It was clear after several sessions with DUSO that there were academic fringe benefits related to the program. These benefits could be classified as language arts, and included listening, thinking, individual self-expression, and group discussion.

The DUSO activities were so well received by the primary II class that I was asked to present the program to the entire group of primary teachers. In order to give adequate detail to the presentation, I found it helpful to list minor themes related to each of the major themes presented in the DUSO manual.

The organization follows:

DUSO: DEVELOPING UNDERSTANDING OF SELF AND OTHERS

Objectives:

1. To help children in the kindergarten and primary classes move toward self-actualization.
2. To help the regular classroom teacher provide regular, coordinated activities which promote self-actualization.
3. To provide educational experiences which foster harmony between affect and cognition in the learning process.

THEMES AROUND WHICH THE PROGRAM IS ORGANIZED

Major Theme #1: Understanding and Accepting Self

Minor Themes:

1. Pride in being me.

2. Differences in people are natural.
3. The reasons for my behavior.
4. When people want to be with me.
5. My responsibility when I feel left out.

Major Theme #2: Understanding Feelings
Minor Themes:

1. The value of sharing.
2. Express your own feelings.
3. Think about the feelings of others.
4. The feeling of being left out.

Major Theme #3: Understanding Others
Minor Themes:

1. The advantages of working together.
2. The responsibility of each person.
3. How to make friends.
4. Encouragement helps.

Major Theme #4: Understanding Independence
Minor Themes:

1. Learning to take care of yourself.
2. Do your best.
3. Developing good work habits.
4. Use your own resources.
5. Understanding the concept of freedom.

Major Theme #5: Understanding Goals and Purposeful Behavior
Minor Themes:

1. Knowing what your achievements are.

2. Build confidence through tackling new tasks.
3. Determination is important in achievement.
4. Try different ways.
5. Be honest with yourself.

Major Theme #6: Understanding Mastery, Competence and Resourcefulness

Minor Themes:

1. Knowing what your achievements are.
2. Build confidence through tackling new tasks.
3. Determination is important in achievement.
4. Try different ways.
5. Be yourself.

Major Theme #7: Understanding Emotional Maturity

Minor Themes:

1. Is there any value in worrying?
2. Changes produce different feelings.
3. Patience is helpful.
4. Help with your troubles.
5. What is responsibility?

Major Theme #8: Understanding Choices and Consequences

Minor Themes:

1. Learn to make an independent decision.
2. Honesty is a good policy.
3. Fair play is a must if the game is to go smoothly.
4. Each person is important.

By dividing a minor theme into subthemes, I was able to demonstrate more opportunities for development. For example:

Major Theme #2: Understanding Feelings

Minor Theme #1: Express your own feelings.
Subthemes:

1. When you are punished.
2. When you are disappointed or frustrated.
3. When you receive good news.
4. When you are lonely.

The presentation of this organization of themes and subthemes served as a stimulus in making the DUSO program a regular activity in primary-unit classrooms. Teachers later reported with great enthusiasm gains in developing acceptance and increasing awareness of self and others, in creating more effective discussions in identifying the DUSO words and, most important, in nurturing respect for and valuing of the uniqueness and incomparable nature of each individual self.

Another resource available to teachers who approach personal development through language arts and reading is the black ABC's series. This program is especially relevant to urban black children. It is a set of twenty-six Picture-Story Study Prints beautifully illustrated in color and designed to help teach children in primary classes recognition of the letters of the alphabet and the speech sounds they represent.

Black ABC's focuses on black children and adults, reflecting their majority position in many parts of big cities and in many city schools. Black ABC's helps black children see themselves as members of a group of capable, attractive, and responsible people with a long history of outstanding contributions in the United States and in the world.

The key words in the Black ABC's are personal words which relate to feelings, aspirations, self-respect, self-pride, and personal goals. They have special meaning for black children:

A is for *a*fro.
B is for *b*eautiful.

C is for *c*ool.

D is for *d*ream.

E is for *e*verybody.

F is for *f*amily.

G is for *g*roovy.

H is for *h*ome.

I is for *i*mportant.

J is for *j*azz.

K is for *k*ids.

L is for *l*earn.

M is for *m*e.

N is for *n*atural.

O is for *o*ld.

P is for *p*roud.

Q is for *q*uick.

R is for *r*ead.

S is for *s*oul *s*ister.

T is for *t*alk.

U is for *u*s.

V is for *v*ote.

W is for *w*ork.

X is for *e*xtra-special.

Y is for *y*oung.

Z is for *z*ip.

On the reverse side each picture print has teaching suggestions which include a way of presenting the letter and the picture; discussion questions about the picture; specific learning activities related to the letter; and enrichment activities. The prints are organized in such a way that the teacher can use his own creative approach in sharing them with children.

A student teacher described the unfolding life in one class-room.

[barbara kezur]

Paper bags rustling.
Ginny and I attempting to show how the bags can be transformed into puppets.
Snatches of conversation: "Ginny, help me." "Barb, what kind of face should I put on my puppet?" "Miss Sumner, I need more newspaper for stuffing."
Smiles, concentrated looks, real involvement on an individual and group level.
Me, hurrying around the room, tearing strips of paper for stuffing, feeling very immersed in the world of children.
Puppet heads beginning to emerge, unique, infinite variety.
Douglas forgetting his shyness in his excitement over his puppet.
Me, feeling good because Miss Sumner, Ginny, and I were all work-ing together.
Puppet show, beginning with lots of fighting, moving away from that into real encounter among the children.
The beauty of Miss Sumner entering the world of her children and becoming a part of it with them.
My own surprise at the created dramas of the children and being in touch with their tremendous expressions in just being.
A feeling of noticeable growth in my relationship with Ginny and Miss Sumner and all the children.
A feeling of fullness and aliveness.

Another student wrote:

[barbara sheedy]

This year at Williams School has been filled with life. There were many ups and downs, and I was often prone to dwell upon the disheartening incidents and to discount the joyful moments as no more than my due. Now, as I am looking back over the year, there are a few moments in time which seem as vivid to me as they were in the actual experiences.

PINK, WITH ORANGE HAIR AND BROWN POLKA DOTS

(discussion after listening to the Sesame Street frog sing about what it's like to be green—first-grade class)

Barbara. Did any of you ever feel the way the frog did? Did you ever want to change the way you look?

Various Children. (after a few moments silence):
I like the way I look.
I want to have a natural look.
I hate the way I look.
I'm gonna look like my daddy when I grow up.

Sandra. (emphatically stopping the chatter): I don't *like* the way I look! I want to look like you! I want to be the same color as you (pointing to me)!

Barbara. (surprised, flustered, but excited by the intensity of feeling and Sandra's freedom to express it): What color am I?

Other Children. (while Sandra is thinking): White!

Sandra. No, she's not white (the other children wait while Sandra tries to decide how to accurately describe my color). She's not white, she's . . . she's pink, with orange hair and brown polka dots.

Barbara. (after a long silence): Why do you want to look like me, Sandra? Is what you look like on the outside more important than the way you feel on the inside?

Other Children. No. It doesn't matter what you look like as long as you're a nice person. God made us all look different so that's the way it should be.

Randy. (effectively ending a discussion which was slowly dying): It doesn't matter what we look like, we're all human beings!

As I write this I realize that I was not really accepting Sandra's feelings. I wanted to change her, to let her know that I like her as she is, regardless of what she wants to be. I am feeling very thankful now; thankful that Sandra helped me to experience (rather than just intellectually acknowledge) the difference between really hearing and accepting the feelings of a person I care for, and trying to make the person be as I would like them to be just because *I* care. I am also thankful that Sandra did not see me in a stereotyped way; I was not white, but pink with orange hair and brown polka dots.

The following experiences struck me as particularly relevant to human values and human education:

[angie hunt]

For the past six months I've been at Williams School—or have I really been there? Was I only there as a physical entity? Yes, there were days when, although my body was there, "I" was not. Yet there have been alive moments, as on Tuesday, when Gloria snuck in a quick kiss right on my lips! My body tingled as the kiss penetrated my anxiety of "losing my cool." What if the children should ignore my desire for order? What if their individuality should infringe upon mine? Yes, I guess these questions were the basis of my anxiety. But Gloria's kiss brought me into the here and now, making the "what ifs" irrelevant.

I like Mrs. C. On Friday, after our scavenger hunt, we colored a mural of all we saw, smelled, touched, heard, and felt along the way. Soon the classroom spontaneously fell into a variety of activities. William, Janice, Johnny, and a few others still were working on the mural. Roland was coloring at a nearby table. Tommy and Belinda were putting letters on the magnetic board. Karl was playing the xylophone. Kevin was finishing yesterday's paper. Daisy was writing on the chalkboard. Laurence was chatting with Rayford. Mrs. C. was taking pictures off the bulletin board in order to make room for the mural. The room looked totally disorganized and, at the same time, sensibly in order. Mrs. C. seemed perfectly comfortable with what was happening. It was one of the most beautiful moments of my year. No words do justice to the overwhelming feeling of . . . of love. Pure, simple, spontaneous, complete harmony!

Gail told me on the way home that she saw Janice hugging Mrs. C. and Mrs. C. responding with warmth. Is this the same person who showed so much rigidity, tenseness, reserve, several months ago?

The children are so beautiful—Karl, Janet, Katherine, Belinda, Daisy, Laurence, Kevin. Today was such a full day, and it just spontaneously happened!

This morning the sun woke me up and my alarm began chiming, "Oh what a beautiful morning," and it was!

"How old are you?" Janice asked me with her hands on her hips.

"Twenty."

"Are you a *lady?*" Janice asked in a tone of disbelief.

"What do you mean?"

"Are you a lady or a girl?"

"What do you think?"

"A little girl?"

"Well, in age I guess I'm closer to being a lady than a little girl, but I enjoy being like a little girl sometimes, too."

"Gee, that's strange!" Janice declared, and we both giggled. After a hug we went our separate ways, each with a huge smile. Janice had captured some of my childishness. I felt light knowing that we both seemed comfortable with feeling both the little girl and the lady aspects of me.

As we read *Goggles,* Belinda proceeded to tell what was about to happen on the next page! When Peter and Archie tricked the big boys in the story, everyone laughed!

We made goggles of our own out of heavy construction paper, clear plastic, and pipe cleaners. The children looked so funny with them on!

"Don't let the big boys take them away from you," I cautioned Laurence as I put them on him.

"I won't. They'll never get my goggles!" Laurence showed me his fists.

"All you need now is a motorcycle, Rayford," I commented.

"Brum . . . mmm . . . mmm. Brum . . . mmm . . . mmm." Rayford tears around the room.

"Angie . . ."

"Yes, Vernita." I turned to her as she handed me a soggy pair of goggles.

"Willy slobbered all over my goggles!" she reported.

The year has come to a close—today I was in my last class at Williams School. As ends are being tied, I realize that I have not tied one single end in my writings here. The journey away from one peak and onto another one has never been accounted for. I cannot wrap all of these peak moments up and tie a neat bow on them now. The loose ends give me room to continue reaching for new peaks.

I left my last classroom at Williams with a song. I'd like to close for tonight with that song. . . .

> We came to school this morning at the crack of dawn.
> In Mrs. J.'s room strange things were going on.
>> Evy, Ivy, Evy-Ivy over
>> Evy in, Ivy out
>> Evy, Ivy over.
>
> Van, Darrell, Aaron, and Gloria were making lots of noise.
> Vicella and Selina were drawing girls and boys.
> And over in the corner where no one else could see
> Renee, Yoland, and Maibryn were drawing quietly.
>> Evy, Ivy, Evy-Ivy over
>> Evy in, Ivy out
>> Evy, Ivy over.
>
> Aaron looked around at Kevin, Kevin looked at me.
> Benjamin hit Helen and Ernest chased Tracy.
> Gwen told us a story that we all tried to hear.
> Robin yawned and Rita talked and Eric stood on his chair.
>> Evy, Ivy, Evy-Ivy over
>> Evy in, Ivy out
>> Evy, Ivy over.
>
> Well that leaves Mark and Alex and I have to mention Steve.
> Gail and I have had a lot of fun this year, but now we have to leave.

> Evy, Ivy, Evy-Ivy over
> Evy in, Ivy out
> Evy, Ivy over!

Not all learning encounters occurred in groups. Throughout the first two years of involvement in the Williams School, there were many person-to-person relations that developed in depth. Often these grew out of initial conflict between a child and an adult, as in the following examples.

RAY AND MARGE

[marge johnson]

Yesterday I was seated on the carpet with a group of children. I was trying to describe an activity some children had asked about. Ray persisted in talking and interfering with my communication. He interrupted me three times, then started wrestling with another child. Finally I reached out, took hold of his wrists and said, "Ray, I'm getting angry at you. I've asked you three times to stop talking, and——"

"Ow, you're hurting me," he screamed.

I said, "Yes, I see that I'm hurting you, and I don't want to do that but I'm also very angry. How do I get you to stop talking long enough so I can explain how this activity can be done?" He didn't answer me; he only looked at the floor. Seeing that he was quiet and knowing within myself that I was not ready to pursue the issue further, I directed my attention to the rest of the children and organized them into small groups for a series of movement experiences.

Today I confronted Ray, restating that I had been angry with him yesterday because he kept interfering. "Ray," I said, "I think you wanted something from me, but I don't know what. I don't understand why you continued talking when I asked you to stop. What do you want from me?"

He blurted out, "Why can't I go to Merrill-Palmer?" Suddenly I understood his belligerence, not only yesterday but also on other occasions.

M. Because Merrill-Palmer is very small, we can only be with a small number of children.

R. I want to know why I can't go.

M. Miss Long and I talked about who we thought would most benefit from going to Merrill-Palmer. We decided that there were other children who needed the experience more than you.

R. What's the matter with the kids that go there?

M. They're having difficulty getting along with themselves and with others.

R. What do they do there?

M. They go to a playroom, where they are free to do what they wish and be who they are.
   PAUSE

M. Ray, what do you think is the matter with them?

R. They're retarded, or something.

M. Do you think there's something the matter with you?

R. I don't know.

M. Can you say what you want from me when you ignore me?

R. I don't know.

M. Perhaps if you think about it between now and the next time I come you can tell me.

R. (with an angry edge in his voice): Why don't you write stories for me anymore?

M. Oh, Ray! I didn't know that's what you wanted. I'll be glad to.

R. I have lots of stories to tell you, and some poems, too!

M. Wonderful, Ray! We can work together tomorrow when I come.

A big smile appeared on his face. I smiled, too, feeling elated that a misunderstanding which had arisen between us had been cleared up and that now we could work together. I had the feeling that he was saying to me, "I was ignoring you because I felt you were ignoring me." I sensed the value of following up an unfinished experience and felt great excitement in just anticipating the new poems and stories we would create together.

KEVIN AND PAUL

[paul bedell]

Kevin is a boy in the third-grade class where I have been working three half-days a week. We had done some things together in a small group early in the year and had had good times with each other, particularly using puppets in dramatic play. But when we were with other children in the classroom, Kevin would often become belligerent with me. He would deliberately antagonize me and would refuse to listen to anything I had to say. I felt a growing gulf between us; our communications were becoming more and more tense. This came to a head one day when there was a substitute teacher. When I arrived in the afternoon Kevin, along with several other boys, was moving destructively around the room. He was teasing girls, trying to pick fights, and making a lot of noise. It was impossible for anyone else to do anything because of his disturbances. Kevin, particularly, was unwilling to stop or even to listen to what I had to say. When I tried to talk with him, he would only mockingly repeat my words as they came out of my mouth. I became very angry and frustrated. He also became angry. The gulf between us seemed impossibly wide. The day ended with heavy and unresolved tensions between us.

The next morning that I was at the school, two days later, I asked Kevin if he would come for a walk with me. Yes, he would. As we walked I told him about the feelings I had had two days before, and that I was particularly disturbed by our not having been able to talk with each other. I asked him if there was something I could do when he got into that belligerent mood so that he would not shut me out. He had no answer for me and quickly changed the subject. A man we had just passed had once killed a white person. He did not like black boys and white men to be walking together.

Later in the walk I said that I felt very friendly toward him at the moment. He said yes, we were friends. "But," I said, "I know and you know that sooner or later another time like the one we had last week is going to come up. We will get angry with each other. Probably we will not be able to talk or listen to each other. When that happens, remember that I am still your friend. I still will like to be with you. When our anger passes we will be able to talk again."

The next time I came another incident occurred. The teacher was out of the room for a few minutes and I was the only adult in the class. Kevin immediately jumped up and began to move about. He and another fellow began to wrestle in angry combat. I stopped the fight, but once again Kevin would not listen to anything I had to say. He was angry with me and I with him. "Now," I said, "this is a time like we were talking about last week. We are angry and we aren't listening to each other. But remember I am still your friend."

He remained sullen and angry toward me for almost an hour longer that morning. He would not talk to me directly, nor would he look at me, but he would keep doing things which showed he wanted contact with me. He would come over and annoy the person with whom I was working, but pointedly ignore me. He came and took my pencil, saying I had stolen it from him. Finally, looking very unhappy and filled with internal struggle, he told the teacher that he would like to speak to me. I came over and he whispered in my ear, "I'm sorry, Paul." Later in the morning, as I was helping him write a story, he looked at my blond hair intently and said with surprise and warmth, "Paul, your hair is turning black. Pretty soon you'll have a natural."

STEVE AND ANNE

[anne breznau]

Steve is an angry, violent first-grade child. Since the beginning of the year he has been pinching, kicking, punching, and really trying to hurt other children in the class. I have seen his face as he pinches someone. It is expressing pleasure and hatred. His dark eyes at those moments are on fire.

Steve is also vividly creative. He finger-paints thunderous, stormy pictures using unusual combinations of various shades of pink and purple with deep grays and blacks. The pictures are never imitative or ordinary—they are wild, imaginative, and purely Steve's own. I am excited about Steve. When I tell him how much I like his pictures and how beautiful I think they are, his eyes glow and shine with pleasure.

One day, we were making Halloween masks out of paper plates, paints, felt, yarn, cotton balls, and any other scraps of things we could find. Steve's mask was painted half fuschia and half black—it was, as usual, completely different and magnificent. Grace looked at the mask and asked him to do another one because the mask didn't have eyes or other features. Unknowingly I walked by and saw his beautiful mask lying on the floor. I knew at once whose it was, and I picked it up and exclaimed at how beautiful I thought it was. Grace was surprised that I liked it and at once called Steve over and said, "Steve, come here. Anne likes your mask so it must be all right." Steve, who cannot cut out simple replicas of what someone else does, often suffers because his creativity is not recognized.

This is all background to a moment that we shared yesterday —actually, it lasted about an hour. Steve exploded yesterday. A fight started and I don't know who was responsible. The important thing is that another boy slapped Steve across the face. I had my back turned when suddenly I heard a piercing shriek not like any scream I have ever heard before. Steve was screaming with his whole heart and voice and then he exploded into violent sobbing and wailing and moaning. The substitute teacher picked him up and was holding him, but she kept saying, "Steve, what's wrong. What's wrong? Where does it hurt?" Finally, she lost patience and said, "Oh, for heaven's sake, what're you crying for?" At that point, I couldn't restrain myself any longer. I went over and sat beside her and eased Steve onto my lap. He was eager to come and he clung to me, sobbing his whole self out, it seemed.

I held Steve as he sobbed and moaned for about a half hour. Then I told him it was about time for me to leave and I asked him if he was ready to be put down. His sobbing had subsided to small moans and whimpers. He nodded. He stood up slowly, and directly in front of him was standing the boy who had slapped him. I looked at Steve and I was frightened. His face was expressing the most pure look of violence and hatred that I have ever seen. I was awed by the purity of his anger. It was like watching a volcano seethe and begin to erupt. It was incredibly moving. I said to Steve after a moment, "Who are you mad at?"

He said, "David."

I said, "What would you like to do to him if you could do anything that you wanted to do?"

He said, "Kill him."

I said, "How would you kill him?"

He said, "I'd stab him."

I said, "Then what would you do?"

He said, "I'd dump him in the garbage!"

David was long gone. One look at Steve's face and he was not about to hang around.

I said, "Would you like to come away with me and beat up something else and pretend it's David?"

He paused. Then, he said, "Yes."

All through the conversation, he was very clear and unhesitating about what he wanted.

I took him over in a corner and piled up a bunch of coats. I told him to pretend these were David and to go ahead and kill them.

He began without hesitation to kick, jump up and down on, throw against the wall, tear at, pound, and in every way try to destroy the coats. He kept doing this for about fifteen minutes. He was utterly oblivious to the other children or anyone else. I think he was conscious of my presence, but his main attention was totally on what he was trying to do. Rage just seemed to pour out of him onto those coats. Eventually he focused on only one coat and he really pounded it. Again, I was frightened that he would never stop, but I knew there was nothing to do except wait for him. Finally, he picked up the coat and threw it against the wall especially hard.

Then he jumped up and down on it. Then he paused. I waited a moment and then said, "Is it dead?"

He said, "Yeah."

I said, "Do you feel better?"

He said, "Yeah."

He then said that he was hungry and got his own coat off the hook. I put my arm around him briefly. I felt his relaxation and better feelings. He went to lunch.

This was one of the most beautiful experiences of my life.

[cereta perry]

MATHEMATICS FOR THE HUMAN CLASSROOM

As I WORKED with Merrill-Palmer students and primary teachers to find human ways of encouraging children to develop interest and skill in mathematics, I recalled some of my hard-nosed colleagues (of some years ago) who insisted that mathematics was intrinsically heavy and demanded severe discipline and concentration. Although I did not agree with this point of view, I was aware that many students avoided math whenever they could. Even so, I strongly believed that there were ways of introducing math to primary classes that would lead to successful achievement and yet be fun. During my search for materials and ideas, I encountered the following statement:

> . . . it is as true of arithmetic as it is of poetry that in some place and at some time it ought to be a good thing to be appreciated on its own account—just as an enjoyable experience in short. If it is not, then when the time and place come for it to be used as a means of instrumentality, it will be just that much handicap. Never having

realized or appreciated mathematics for itself, one will miss something of its capacity as a resource for other ends. . . .[1]

As I got in touch with the meaning of these words, I was able to go back into my experience and recreate the situation of a group of happy little five-year-old girls jumping rope and chanting:

1   2   buckle my shoe
3   4   shut the door
5   6   pick up sticks
7   8   lay them straight
9   10 do it again

What were these children learning relative to mathematics? First and foremost, they were developing a positive attitude toward numbers; they were integrating numbers, rhythms, and physical activity. These scenes of young children counting rhythmically urged me to explore resources that would contribute to the development of children joyfully engaged in learning mathematics. Keeping in mind that teachers were concerned with specific concepts they were expected to teach, I requested the mathematics course of study of the Detroit Public Schools for primary grades.[2] This course of study listed a number of objectives for primary grades.

A child should:

I. *By the end of the kindergarten year*
   a. identify a set.
   b. recognize numerals zero to nine.
   c. relate one-to-one matching.
   d. identify a circle, a square and a triangle.

II. *By the end of primary one*
   a. tell the value of coins through the dime.
   b. show the "greater than" and "less than" concepts with sets of objects.

[1] John Dewey, *Democracy and Education* (New York: The Free Press, 1930), p. 240.
[2] Detroit Public Schools, "Mathematics, Minimum Standards" (Detroit Board of Education, Detroit, Michigan).

c. count with meaning by associating objects with numerals and by using the concept of place value.

d. join sets to show the operation of addition.

e. add one to a number up to nine without using sets of objects.

f. write the addition combination up to the sum of five, using sets of objects.

g. subtract one from a number up to nine, using sets of objects.

h. name the elementary geometrical figures (circle, rectangle, square, triangle).

III. *By the end of primary two*

a. use the commutative property of addition for the addition combinations he has learned.

b. write addition facts (sums of ten) for picture stories of sets.

c. write numerals using place value for counting numbers one through ninety-nine. He will use sets of objects to show the meaning of any numeral.

d. perform the operation of addition and its inverse subtraction in word problems.

e. relate time with the use of the clock for the hour and half hour.

f. relate time with the use of the calendar.

g. relate the value of money through the quarter.

IV. *By the end of grade three*

a. use place value for writing numerals.

b. group and re-group objects to show

5 hundreds	4 tens	3 ones =
4 hundreds	14 tens	3 ones =
4 hundreds	13 tens	3 ones =

c. discover the operation of multiplication as repeated addition of the same number.

d. indicate his knowledge of simple multiplication facts to threes.

e. write different fractions for different drawings.

f. explain the meaning of a fraction.

g. relate standard units of measurement as:

clock—hours, half hour, quarter hour

calendar—date, day

ruler—inches, foot, yard

    h. read simple bar and line graphs
    i. draw the following geometrical figures:
        line segment
        line
        ray
        point
        circle
        square
        rectangle
        pentagon
        triangle

The course of study as outlined was flexible enough to enable us to develop a formula that proved effective in fulfilling the objectives. Four key words were joined: NUMERALS plus MUSIC plus MOVEMENT plus COLORS. Through these we created ways for children to appreciate arithmetic "on its own account—just as an enjoyable experience."

I found it helpful to keep a few principles in focus as I designed a series of math activities to help teachers introduce increasingly complex arithmetic concepts and skills.

1. A pleasant, success-oriented program enhances the child's self-esteem.
2. Content relevant to the life of the learner fosters self-motivated involvement.
3. Encouraging different solutions to the same problem recognizes that each child has his own learning style.
4. Gradual enlarging of concepts and skills, recognizing each child's pace, contributes to a child's commitment and desire to learn.

Some projects that we developed in our effort to humanize mathematics are described below.

MY PERSONAL BOOK OF NUMBERS

This activity is appropriate as a method of introducing children to numerals, developing awareness, and contributing to the recognition of each numeral, to the ability to reproduce it, and to an understanding of the numeral's meaning.

The teacher and the children assemble materials of many different textures (construction paper, cardboard, sandpaper, oilcloth, plastic, etc.). A variety of colors and textures enrich working with the materials. Children should be encouraged to explore fully all the materials and decide which materials and which colors offer the most exciting possibilities for making numerals.

The teacher remains available to help children, if requested, as they assemble numbers in their books.

Interest is expanded when the child is free to select his favorite number and to create a story about that number.

A child takes great pride in his own creation. Self-direction and self-affirmation are important ingredients in real learning.

NUMBERS IN MY COMMUNITY

When the child has become familiar with numerals, he can move on to enlarge his perceptual field. His community is an immediate and important resource for this activity.

A suggested beginning is with the child's house number. Moving from this point, the child might be invited to participate in a survey. Each child can count and report the number of stores, churches, other business establishments, families, etc., in the neighborhood.

The child will probably suggest additional items to be included in the survey.

DANCING NUMERALS

One delightful find in my exploration of resources was the record *Dancing Numerals*.[3] With the aid of this record children developed

[3] Rosemary Hallum, et al., "Dancing Numerals" AR537 (Freeport, New York: Educational Activities, Inc.).

many of the necessary math concepts as they joyfully participated in the music, games, and charts. The concepts included in the record are recognition of numerals, simple counting (in order and in reverse order), counting by twos, threes, fours, fives, sixes, sevens, eights, nines, tens, hundreds, and thousands, developing sets, joining of sets, addition, subtraction, geometric figures, numerical value, and monetary value.

The catchy tunes and the movements made this a popular resource. All the teachers in our project used this record as a stimulus in creating additional math experiences for children.

THE SINGING MULTIPLICATION TABLES

MMM—Mathematics, Music, and Movement. This collection of records enables the teacher to dispense with the presentation of the multiplication tables through rote memory.[4] The records present the tables from two through twelve with varying, catchy rhythms. The rhythms encourage the child to move in clear, definite rhythmical patterns and to create movement pictures which may be shared with others.

FIRST THINGS: MATHEMATICS

The new math emerged after teachers currently in primary classrooms had mastered the traditional or old math. Presenting the new math in exciting, stimulating ways was a chore for many. The program "First Things" Mathematics was my response to teachers' requests for help in this area.[5] The program includes six full-color,

[4] Hap Palmer, *Singing Multiplication Tables: From the 2's through the 12's.* Album 45-101-6-45 rpm records (Freeport, New York: Educational Activities, Inc.).

[5] Guidance Associates, *First Things: Mathematics. Sound Strips for Primary Years* (Pleasantville, New York).

sound filmstrips with a manual accompanying each filmstrip. The filmstrips present, in a dramatic way, the concepts comprising the new math and offer suggestions for the development of creative activities related to the concept. The organization of the filmstrips follows.

1. *Making sense of sets*
    a set
    equivalent sets
    nonequivalent sets

2. *More about sets*
    relationship of number to sets
    subsets
    an empty set

3. *Measurement: how to say how much*
    units of length
    units of weight
    units of volume

4. *Beginning geometry*

point	end point
line	triangle
line segments	rectangle
square	

5. *Comparison: putting a symbol to work*
    equal $=$
    unequal $\neq$
    less than $<$
    greater than $>$

6. *Number patterns: puzzles with a purpose*
    logical mathematical thinking

Use of the filmstrips seemed to release the creative potential of teachers and students, and many unique activities resulted as the children absorbed and integrated the knowledge.

Our facilitation of the learning of math in a human way, using movement, music, and art, intensified and expanded the cooperative spirit between the Williams School staff and the Merrill-Palmer faculty and students.

A detailed example of how one student approached linear measurement and developed linear concepts with meaning illustrates a process used with many of our math activities.

[al rodriguez]

My task here is to relate how certain traditional goals were achieved in a humanistic setting. While personal and academic knowledge were both ongoing in this classroom, I am focusing primarily on a process that leads to a meaningful understanding of specific academic concepts. The learning situation blossoms into its fullest potential when interaction between the participants is authentic, the atmosphere is human, and the concepts are concretely experienced.

I developed a series of activities that brought elementary children into a real encounter with linear measurement. More specifically, in concrete ways I introduced concepts of inch, foot, yard, and mile, and the usage of these concepts in measuring objects. I invited each child to approach his physical self, his body, from the single dimension of linear distance. This process recognizes the child's capacity to become personally involved in sharing in the unfolding of a meaningful experience.

The preparatory experience (presented to the entire classroom) included an introduction to linear measurement through mathematical filmstrips,[6] available in our unit program at Merrill-Palmer. A brief question-and-answer period followed which centered on the units of inch, foot, yard, and mile.

> Can anyone show me how much an inch is? Have you ever seen anyone measure something in inches? Who was the person? What was the person using to measure the object? How did the person measure the object? What did he do?

[6] "Measurement: How to Say How Much." *First Things: Mathematics. Sound Filmstrips for Primary Years* (Guidance Associates of Pleasantville, New York).

Does anyone know how much a foot is? Show me how long a foot is with your hands. Is that longer or shorter than an inch? Find an object in the classroom that you can measure in inches. Find an object in the classroom that you can measure in feet. What parts of your body can you measure in inches? What parts of your body can you measure in feet?

How much is a yard? Show me. Have you ever heard of anything measured in yards? What was the object? Is a yard longer than a foot? How about an inch?

The unit of a mile was discussed with reference to the distance that each child lived from the school. For example, Joseph's house was approximately three-quarters of a mile from school. He had to leave his house earlier than any other child to get to school at 9:00 A.M. because he had to walk farther.

In the next session, the classroom teacher and I divided the children into two groups with approximately twelve students in each group. After discussing the limits in our group activity, I probed the children to find out if they understood the relationship between inch and foot.

Miller, can you tell me what this is? Does anyone know what it is? Has anyone seen someone use it? Have you ever used this, Katrina? Yes, it is a ruler. What kind of ruler is it? An inch? A foot? A yard? Can you show me how much an inch is with your fingers? Is the length of this ruler the same length as an inch? Is it the same length as a foot? What do these little black marks and numbers mean? How much is it from the end of the ruler to the line with the number "1" near it? Can you make the same distance with your fingers? Now make the distance of an inch. Yes, they're both the same. How many of these inch distances are on the ruler? How many inches are there in a foot? Is the foot the same size as twelve of these inch units? Let's count them again.

Next, I invited each child to search the classroom and bring back an object that was an inch long. We discussed each object in terms of what it was and its distance in inches. We accepted only those objects which were either an inch long or an inch wide. To demonstrate that the numbers on the ruler represent the sum of an object's inch units, I directed the children to line up their objects in a chain. Each child knew that his object was an inch in distance. Two objects then linked together were two inches. I asked, "What is the number printed on the ruler nearest to the end of our second object?" I continued the procedure until the series of objects distanced twelve inches. "How long is our chain of objects? One foot or twelve inches?" To test if the children understood the relationship between the printed numbers and the sum of inch units, I randomly broke off the chain and asked, "How long is our chain of objects now?" Then I asked a number of individual children to make the chain an x-amount of inches in distance. This was repeated many times.

The next session dealt with acquainting each child with the fundamentals of measuring.

> Now, I would like each of you to go back to your desk and bring back a pencil or a crayon to draw with. Lamar, would you also bring back sheets of green drawing paper for everyone.
> Let's sit in our circle while we wait for everyone to come back.
> I cannot talk when everyone is talking, so I will wait a couple of minutes for you to finish up whatever you want to say. I really want to continue because we are going to measure something very interesting, something that none of you have ever measured before.
> I am going to divide you into four groups with four people in each group.
> Now that your groups are established, I would like each of you to draw a picture of yourself.

After each child completed his drawing, I gave the following directions:

> Here are rulers for each group. Can you measure the different parts of your body? If you want to, you can work all together or in pairs. I will visit each group and help you with any problems you are encountering.

With each of the small groups, I asked the following questions:

> What person are you measuring now? What part of her body are you measuring? From where to where on her body are you measuring?

If the group needed direction in measuring, I first asked, "Would you like me to help you with what you are doing?" If anyone needed help, I gave the person a specific responsibility. For example, in measuring the length of Curtis' body, Dennis showed from which two points we were going to measure. Dennis held two rulers (one on top of another lengthwise) while Venzetta connected two more foot rulers. Melissa stood on a chair and added a fifth ruler which went beyond the length of Curtis' body. Melissa was also responsible for finding the number that was closest to the top of Curtis' head. Curtis, during the measuring, was responsible for keeping his body as rigid and straight as possible, being careful not to move the slightest fraction. Melissa told the number of inches that were on the last ruler and we added on the number of feet represented by the other four rulers. Curtis was four feet and five inches. I then showed Curtis how to make arrows on his drawing to represent the distance we measured. With the group's assistance he wrote down the numerals and the unit labels for the length of his body. The same procedure was followed for measuring others in the group; the measurement roles were rotated. This collective effort ended our preparatory experience.

Benjamin, Miller, Katrina, Paulette, today I'm going to be working exclusively with you in the cloakroom. We will be making a life-size poster outline of someone's body and labeling the different parts in inches and feet. Before we start, I would like to talk with you about the limits that will be necessary for you to work within if I am to be with you. Why don't we sit around in a circle so everyone can see each other? Tell me, what are the things you think we won't be able to do?

Miller: Not everyone talks.

Al: Why not?

Miller: Because no one can hear.

Al: Yes, I also get confused when everyone is talking at once because I can't really hear what each person is saying. I also don't like to be interrupted when I am talking to someone. I would prefer that you hold your questions or comments until the person and I are finished. I, in return, will not interrupt when two other people are having a conversation.

Okay, quietly go back to your desks and bring back your crayons. If you don't have any, borrow some from a friend. Katrina, would you also bring the rulers.

I would like all of you to decide amongst yourselves who is going to be outlined. We only have time enough to do two people today and there are four of you. I am going to get the paper and materials ready. I'll come back when you have made the decision of who is to be drawn.

Have you come to a decision yet?

How did you come to your decision? Katrina, do you agree that Benjamin and Paulette are to be outlined? Miller, do you agree that Benjamin and Paulette are to be outlined?

Who's first?

What's this? Yes, it's a ruler, a foot ruler. What is it used for? How can one measure with it? What are these lines and numbers for? Does anyone remember how much an inch is? Can you do it with your hands? And a foot, how much is that? How long would one foot and one inch be? Katrina, can you be the foot and Miller, can you be the inch? Let's put them together.

What color shall we use to outline Benjamin?

Benjamin, lie down on this paper and place your body in just the way you want to be outlined. Make every part of your body stiff now, every muscle, your head, neck, shoulders, arms, hands, fingers, chest, stomach, thighs, knees, calves, ankles, feet, toes. Everything stiff like cardboard so we can trace around it. Make your body heavy so it can't be moved.

Everyone else, carefully, lightly trace slowly around his body. Try not to move anything except the crayon you are using.

Benjamin, we are finished. When you feel like getting up, we can continue with the rest of our project.

Let's all make the lines real dark now so we can see the whole outline.

Benjamin, what part of your body would you like to measure? How are you going to measure it?

Benjamin lined up the rulers beginning at the heel and stopping when the rulers had passed the head of his outline.

How many complete rulers do you have laid down? And how many inches of the one that isn't complete? How tall is your outline in feet and inches? That's right, how did you figure that out?

Now, I'll draw an arrow from the tip of his heel and another arrow from the tip of his head. What is the space between the two arrows for? Can you write in feet and inches how long the outline is? Does anyone know how to spell *feet?* Does anyone know how to spell *inches?*

Now each of you can find a part that interests you and measure it.

The children proceeded to measure parts of Benjamin's body.

Paulette, can I measure part of the outline with you?

Does anyone see a part of the outline that we haven't measured yet? Let's do it!

Everyone ready to color?

Benjamin, there is a mirror on that desk. You can use that to see what your face looks like, then you can shape and color what it looks like to you.

The rest of us will color the other parts. I think I'll color the left shoe.

Does anyone feel that the picture needs more coloring? Why don't we stop then.

Here are some tacks I found. Where do you think we can tack our picture up? I really like it.

How tall is Benjamin according to this outline? Where does it say that? What do those arrows mean?

What part did you measure, Katrina? How did you measure it? How wide is his hand? Did you use the foot unit? What two points did you measure from?

Our group decided to limit the discussion of the finished outline of Benjamin until we had completed the outline for Paulette. The same procedures were used for Paulette's outline. We tacked both outlines up and discussed how they differed. I invited each child to share with us the part that he had measured. While looking at the crude outlines and seeing the look of pride and accomplishment on the children's faces, I felt certain that they had learned what measurement was all about.

The perspective that I have been writing from is limited. Mathematical concepts were only part of the experience. Creativity, personal and honest interaction, joy, self-awareness, group collectiveness, sharing, involvement, self-expression, caring—these human qualities were reflected in every session. Life had been created in the classroom with learning that was alive and exciting. The children were fully involved, valuing and seeking what they were learning, enjoying the process, and not wanting it to end.

[clark moustakas]

THE PLAY-THERAPY PROGRAM

WITHIN THE FIRST THREE MONTHS of our involvement in the Williams Shcool, we became aware of individual children who, though responsive to many of the projects we were developing, required a special relationship, difficult to create in depth in the classroom. In consultation with teachers and the school counselor, and with the consent of parents and the principal of the school, we began our work in play therapy with these children. In general, the group represented two extremes: hostile, abrasive, and often destructive children in trouble with peers, teachers, and administrators; and children who were extremely withdrawn, isolated, and almost totally nonresponsive to others. The majority of the children referred were in the latter grouping. Because we had ample space, materials, and equipment as well as observational facilities for supervision of our students, we decided to meet the children at The Merrill-Palmer Institute. Initially our main problem was transportation; parents often agreed to bring their children to Merrill-Palmer but did not fulfill these commitments, claiming last-minute emergencies and other pressing matters. Therefore, we switched the program to the

Williams School, where we were assigned a room. This change proved to be an even more frustrating experience. The only available room was also used by other special teachers and for handling extreme behavior. Often the room was occupied during our scheduled hours, and our sessions had to be delayed. Many times we were interrupted by people coming to get materials from the room. The interruptions of the sessions and interference with the schedule were continuous, so we abandoned our play-therapy efforts at the school. Once again we returned to the Merrill-Palmer playrooms. With the assistance of the Merrill-Palmer administration, and with the help of volunteers and our own Merrill-Palmer students, we set up a program that proved to be an essential adjunct to our work in the classrooms. Through a number of frustrating disappointments, we eventually found a way of fitting our schedule to the child's pattern of school attendance. Children who were more apt to be absent on Mondays and Fridays were scheduled on other days. In one instance, when a child didn't come to school for a stretch of time his teacher drove to his home and delivered him to Merrill-Palmer.

The play-therapy program became the highlight of the child's week. And, as the play sessions were eagerly anticipated, we were soon deluged by other children at the school with requests and demands to be allowed to come to Merrill-Palmer. Although we met with only twenty children in play therapy (this represented about two-thirds of the total number referred), we brought many of the other children to Merrill-Palmer in small groups, often to view themselves on the video tapes that we made at the school. Our own students regarded their involvement in play therapy as a key opportunity for training and growth. Cereta and I were jointly responsible for supervision. We met with our students weekly and sometimes observed the sessions. The philosophy, methods, and materials, as well as the supervisory process, have been previously discussed (in my book *Psychotherapy With Children*)[1] and thus will not be included here.

At first, though the teachers were supportive of the program, they did not become very much involved in it. But as the children's

[1] Clark Moustakas, *Psychotherapy With Children* (New York: Harper and Row, 1959).

experience of therapy began to influence their behavior in the class-room, teachers sought special times to discuss the process. They requested a reading list, and during a series of lunch meetings we discussed the functions, values, and goals of play therapy. Some teachers wanted to observe, but we felt that this violated the child's right to a private experience and did not grant permission. We sug-gested a demonstration session of a real situation, but the teachers felt they had gained sufficiently from reading and discussion.

From the response of school staff and from the children's as-sessment, we came to see the play-therapy program as an important aid in dealing with severe conflicts and behavior disorders. To cap-ture the flavor of the process, the nature of the relationships devel-oped, and the outcome of individual sessions, several examples are presented below. These illustrations represent lives in process rather than closed or finalized experiences.

GLORIA AND CAROLYN

[carolyn veresh]

When I met Gloria at the Williams School for the first time and spoke to her about coming to Merrill-Palmer, she said nothing to me. She was still and contained; her only visible response was a quiet, quick look into my eyes. There was a long silence—a very sobering thing for me. Immediately, doubts raced through my mind. Would I be able to live with long periods of silence and let her be? I knew I could not push, but did I have the patience to live with her in her way?

JANUARY 17

"Gloria, this is your time to do what you want, there are lots of toys in here. If you want, you can play with them, but you don't have to do anything you don't want to." The quietness and stillness was something I had never before experienced with a child. For some time, I felt calm and peaceful inside. I was surprised at how long that stayed with me, and then I began to recognize a fleeting feeling of impatience. It was just a slight stirring of wanting her to do something. I really got in touch with this feeling and realized clearly that it was *I* who wanted action; it was *I* who felt uncomfortable. Once I got in touch and realized what was happening in me, I grew calmer, more peaceful.

After a time, Gloria slowly moved toward the puppet box. I felt she was struggling to initiate play, but was having trouble finding the courage to act alone. She picked up one of the puppets and played with it a moment. Slowly, I picked one, too, and said, "I'm glad to see you, Gloria." Gloria smiled at me. She put down the puppet and so did I. The silence continued. I said nothing more during our time together, except to tell her at 1:55 that we had five minutes left. After the play with the puppets, Gloria did not move for a long time. Then, slowly, she played briefly with the cash register, the dolls, and the sandbox. I was feeling Gloria struggling very hard during our time together. I felt her nervous, scared, uncertain. I did not want to push her or take responsibility for her acts. She would have to find the strength within herself. I wanted to be with her while she struggled, but I did not feel I could "help" her. Because of these feelings I felt that her play with the other items came from a choice within herself. This was a sobering hour for me, but I felt really good inside. I felt I had stayed in touch with myself and with Gloria. I also felt there was much to learn. I had lots of questions in me that I would be searching into in the coming week.

JANUARY 24
   Gloria was absent.

JANUARY 31
   This was a difficult session for both of us. Gloria froze halfway through a step as the door closed. I waited. She did not move for the longest time. Then slowly she began fidgeting with her clothes; her eyes darted anxiously around the room. I asked if she would like to play with the dolls. Immediately, I felt I shouldn't have said that, but wasn't sure why. A few minutes passed and I said, "If you need to use the bathroom, it's (pointing) over there." Gloria went into the bathroom. She emerged and froze by the dart board. The

silence was really something for me; I could feel waves of uneasiness slowly drift in and out of me. I did not know what to do, so I tried to focus on my feelings. As I grew aware of what was happening inside me, I could distinguish my own needs and feelings from Gloria's. I was still unsure how to communicate my feelings without pushing her, yet I wanted her to know that I, too, was struggling to take the journey in her way. After our time was up, I felt more confidence, but many things were still unsettled for me.

February was disappointing; Gloria was absent every Monday of the month. I talked with Mrs. Massey, the school counselor, and Mrs. Smith, Gloria's mother, and the outcome was to change her appointment to Thursdays.

MARCH 9

Once more, our meeting began with a long period of silence. Today I was even more uncomfortable with the silence, so I initiated an activity and invited Gloria to join me. I felt more comfortable when she was active, but I knew I was out of touch with her. I was very upset with myself after this session because I felt I had escaped the discomfort, that I had not permitted Gloria to stay with the anxiety, to set the pace. I just felt hollow inside, and even as I write this the tears of sadness and frustration cloud my eyes and choke and strain in my throat. I am determined to be with her in a fresh way, somehow to facilitate her in finding a way to a creative, expressive life. I believe I can begin again and let her own rhythm, her own desire to relate, grow from within.

LARRY AND PAUL

[paul bedell]

I have seen Larry eight times to date. No Monday have we missed being together. Though each session has followed a typical pattern, a progression in our relationship and in his use of the playroom is apparent. Each week he has entered our hour with more enthusiasm and confidence. His activities have become more purposeful and show a continuity from one week to the next. He is beginning to verbalize more, and to show more emotion in his facial expression.

During an hour he will usually wrestle for about twenty to thirty minutes with the Bobo, an inflated person-like toy. Over the weeks he has become more and more exuberant in this until now he is quite out of breath after twenty minutes. Recently, after a bout, he went to the blackboard and wrote "I can win Happy Bobo." He seemed especially pleased with himself.

Two weeks ago I decided to consider with him the possibility of terminating, for it seemed to me his activities in the playroom were healthily aggressive, and the manipulation and sneakiness he had exhibited in the classroom had ceased. When I tried to initiate a conversation about his attitude toward coming, and possibly stopping, he became very uncomfortable and began to talk about what he was going to do the next week. His discomfort, and mine, seemed to indicate that we had a way further to go with each other. The last two sessions have shown this indeed to be the case, for our interactions were richer than ever before. I see the sessions now to be opportunities for him to develop the intellectual and emotional sides of his life. I see the same opportunities for myself. We may be entering a rich and fertile field.

MARGO AND SUZANNE

[suzanne toaspern]

I have seen Margo four times to date. I first met her when I visited her classroom. I was a little nervous, and excited, too. I said hello and told her my name and when she would be coming to Merrill-Palmer. She said nothing and looked very sad.

I felt eager and nervous before our first therapy session. This was a special day for me and I felt lonely in the awareness: "No one else really knows how important this day is for me." From my first awakening that morning at dawn's light I throbbed with excitement anticipating my beginning experience as a play therapist. When Margo came for our meeting she didn't look sad, just a little shy. In the playroom she explored many things, starting at one side and moving from item to item with lots of interest. She painted, played a long time with the dishes, and role-played family scenes. I watched her, tried to be in her world. The room was very silent. One or two times I commented on her activities, but she didn't respond. I was surprised at how shy I felt with her, how hard it was for me to convey my understanding of the feelings she expressed. The time went very fast. Margo was continually busy. My words "It's time to go" sounded loud, and startled me in the quiet of the room. I felt satisfied with the first session. I felt I had learned a little about Margo. I wasn't bothered by the silence; it felt calm and seemed natural for a new relationship. As the hour ended, I think both Margo and I were self-absorbed.

My second session with Margo was much like the first. She came eagerly into the room and began to play with the cash register. She explored some new items and also played with things she had used the time before. Margo expressed strong feelings during this hour. She beat on the drums for a long time, with determination, strength, seriousness. I really felt the force of her beating, louder and louder until she reached a rhythm that was also the beat of her life. She spent time punching the punching bag and knocking over toy Indians. I still felt frustrated by my shyness. It still was a great effort to put her feelings into words: "You look angry" or "It feels good and strong when you beat that drum." At times, it felt scary to make a direct statement of how I experienced Margo's feelings. I guess I am afraid that I will interpret her feelings incorrectly— really that wouldn't be so horrid! Margo did not respond to my questions. Only once did she speak, asking me to tie on her boxing glove. We smiled at each other several times. I remember feeling good about the hour when it was over, and thinking that we had communicated more significantly this time. I also remember my resolve to try again to focus on Margo's feelings and to reflect these feelings back to her.

Margo seemed restless when she came into the playroom on the third week. The feelings inside her made her jump from thing to thing with a nervous, hurried, worried look. I pondered a long time on what specific word to attach to this feeling but I could not come up with a clear reaction—so I said nothing. I felt bad for saying nothing; I realized later that I might have said "You seem restless to me" or "Some big feeling's inside you today." As the hour passed Margo became less restless and the session unfolded much like the previous ones. Except for some eye contact and the smiles between us, we did not communicate at all. Then with just five minutes left in the hour, Margo got out the little kitty puppet. Without pondering, I spontaneously picked up a little man puppet and began talking to her through him. It was so much easier for me to talk. I felt for the first time that we were really together. Margo relaxed as our puppet talk continued. Her puppet waved to my puppet and whispered in my puppet's ear. I talked through my puppet, saying, "You are sometimes a quiet kitty aren't you—that's okay with me, I'm sometimes quiet, too. We have lots of time to talk or not. I will always be ready to listen." It felt good to talk with Margo. I felt we really came close to each other. I left thinking, "Wow, this was play therapy for Margo!" Yet as I experienced so much myself I realized how hard it is to share myself, what's really inside, with others. During this time I know that I, too, am learning and growing.

My fourth session with Margo was very exciting. First thing, Margo went to the box with puppets. She took the kitty puppet for herself and gave me the little man. I said "Hello" and she answered "Hello." I asked her questions about school and how she felt there. She said that sometimes she felt happy and sometimes sad. I asked her when was she sad. She said, "When there is no one to help me." The puppets made it easier for both of us to share. Sometimes when Margo talked through her puppet, she would hide her head in her arm and look shy. We talked and played together most of the hour. Margo asked me to play basketball with her and punch the Bobo clown. We also talked on the phone with our puppets. During one phone conversation she asked, "What kind of toys do you have where you live, little man?" I named a few and said that she probably knew about the toys because she had come to the room several times. She said "Yes" and named some more toys. Then she said, "I come here every Thursday, I would like to come every day." I said, "You like it here," and she answered, definitely, "Yes!" It felt good to know she liked coming to Merrill-Palmer, to see me. It felt especially good that we had come together, that we were conversing comfortably and easily. I was beginning to know what it was like to be deeply related to a child from inner self to inner self.

WALT AND TOM

[tom barrett]

Walt tends to be quite cautious in his play. Each week he seems to need about twenty minutes or so to re-explore the playroom and the toys before he can become meaningfully involved. When he does, it's usually in a very elaborate manner. He develops extensive, complicated maneuvers that he acts out. For example, a couple of weeks ago he had the army men execute an attack on the animals. Each man was first of all strategically placed, then advanced, and then the attack took place. The largest wooden horse was subsequently killed in the battle. The other animals were outraged and the army men retreated to their secret hiding place. Next, the animals got together with all of the town people for a joint effort. Each animal was systematically assigned a rider which fit on his back just right. Slowly, then, the animals and riders lined up in single file and advanced in search of the army men's hideout. The army men, however, were all waiting, and ambushed them, killing them all, people and animals alike. This whole procedure took about half an hour and it is a typical example of how long Walt will stay with one thing once he decides the theme and focus of his play.

Not once in the many times I've been with Walt has he initiated a conversation in the playroom. He will usually answer me if I ask a question, but it is always with as few words as necessary, and in a very soft voice. Walt has never expressed any angry feelings directly to me, nor has he laughed or even smiled. At times I really think that my being in the playroom makes no difference at all to him and that he wouldn't notice if I got up and walked out.

In one session we spent at least half the time putting together a band. Walt set up all the drums and cymbals and I played the chimes. We played for several minutes but he still expressed no feelings about the experience. When I asked him if he liked it, he was turned off by my question and withdrew.

Simply stated, Walt seems to be ambivalent toward me and toward our relationship, although he does enjoy coming to Merrill-Palmer and playing. Each week I tell myself that maybe something will happen to bring us closer, but it hasn't, yet. I've tried not saying anything, and I've tried confronting him directly with how I'm feeling, but neither way has been effective. But, at the same time, I'm not sure I know what my real feelings are. At times I wonder if my anxiety is because I'm pushing for some change in him and not just being with him. That is the issue I plan to be more in touch with in our next session.

RON AND TOM

[tom barrett]

Up to about a month ago my relationship with Ron was a totally stagnant one. I think this was because I was doing too much interpreting and not enough paying attention to what I was feeling. Finally everything just exploded in one session and we met head-on. I told him how I felt about what he had been doing and how it made me feel about him. I told him I thought he was pretending to be a big, tough guy and that he was afraid to let himself be kind and gentle with people. I also told him I felt sad that he had always had to be the tough guy, that he couldn't just relax and be himself. We encountered for several minutes. At first, as I kept telling him how I felt, he would try to talk louder than I or cover his ears or just laugh it off. But as he did each of these things I kept pointing out to him that this just proved all the more that he knew it was the truth and that he really was afraid to be nice to people.

Finally we both fell silent, exhausted and drained by the experience. We spent the last ten minutes of the hour just sitting together without saying a word.

Since that time our sessions have changed quite a bit. We've spent two or three of the hours studying about snakes from books and making clay models of them. On the whole, Ron seems to feel freer to express what is inside of him. He seems calmer and is able to stay with one thing for a longer time without feeling a need to act out. Even his teacher, Mrs. Lanier, has commented to me about the change she sees in Ron. Just last week he spent an entire day working on decorating a bulletin board in the classroom. He took a lot of responsibility for the project and helped organize the efforts of the other boys working on it.

To sum up the new direction that the therapy has taken, I would say that Ron seems to be discovering how it feels to be free to be his many-faceted self. He is finding out that it's okay to be gentle sometimes and explosive and energetic at other times. He is finding out that it is okay to really get into something and stay with it, no matter what others around him are doing.

CURTIS AND CAROLYN

[carolyn veresh]

Curtis has a big, beautiful smile, and a cheerful voice that said to me, "Hi! Sure, see you Monday." Walking back into the classroom I could hear him shouting, "I get to go to Merrill-Palmer!" Our first meeting was exciting, a special kind of high.

JANUARY 24

There we were, face to face in the playroom. I was feeling warm and peaceful, ready to face and encounter the realities of our relationship as it began to unfold. My calmness gradually shifted as he talked and moved from one thing to another with the same object in mind: KILL BOBO, KILL BOBO! BANG! POP! POP! POP! A

RIGHT JAB, A LEFT JAB! and now to finish him off, a STAB with the sword, and a slashing, stabbing attack with the knife. I was really tired staying with him. He was beaming: Wow! That sure felt good to get that out!

JANUARY 31

Our next meeting began with a request before we ever reached the playroom. "I want to box with you." "Okay, but I can last only about ten minutes." We boxed vigorously, intently, for the set amount of time. By then I was tired and my lip a little sore from Curtis' left hook. Not so for him. The pop gun was loaded and Bobo received the brunt of his wrath. Slowly the anger was abating and Curtis breathed more calmly. We ended with a game of checkers. It was a relaxing kind of sharing for both of us.

FEBRUARY 7

I was growing more and more eager for our meeting as each new week came. Our smiles were warm and conveyed our feeling of joy more fully than our words. He began to share some thoughts and feelings on fighting. He fought, but not without fear. "Fighting can be pretty scary and hard to do sometimes," Curtis said. He declared, however, that he had no choice when he was fighting with enemies. He hesitated, we both held our breath, and I slowly, quietly said, "Sometimes I fight with my friends and family, too." Curtis responded, "Well, I get *mad* at my friends—even my brothers, too, we fight." I shared with him the feeling of confidence that comes when two friends work out a disagreement. He was unsure of that idea, he would have to try it first. Curtis started, "But——" again a deep breath, fidgeting with his hands, and cautious, darting glances. He seemed to be struggling with whether he should say the thought on the tip of his tongue. It never came. This was a difficult session; we both had struggled with how fully we wanted to share.

FEBRUARY 14

When Curtis did not show up for his therapy appointment I was disappointed and concerned as to why he had not come. I visited him at school the next day and confronted him. He was clearly struggling hard to form the words to tell me that he preferred being with Paul Bedell on the days that Paul came to the school. He also told me he'd rather be with a man in the playroom. A chill of disappointment and rejection ran through me, but still I said that if he chose not to continue working with me, I would accept his decision. However, I added, I would consider it a loss. After a lengthy silence between us, I asked him if he would be willing to put our meetings on a trial basis. We agreed to two more sessions, after which he would decide if he wanted to continue.

FEBRUARY 21

We greeted each other in a serious way but there was joy in the meeting. During the hour, we shared many feelings about our physical characteristics. We shared our thoughts and feelings about coming together, Curtis all the while struggling to accept me. The last part of the hour dealt with fighting. Curtis talked again of his feelings about fighting, allowing me to see the hurt and pain in his eyes and hear the tension and conflict in his voice. "I don't like it, most of the time I feel bad and I want it to stop. Could they come here with me?" There was urgency in his voice and I reassured him that if it was necessary for him to resolve his conflict with others in this way, yes, we could invite them to come. I also told him that although I would stand by him, he would have to be the one to solve the problems he was having with other boys. We both felt good after this meeting and when we parted we smiled, inside and out.

FEBRUARY 28

By the end of February, much of Curtis' hostile behavior had diminished. There were fewer war games and Bobo received fewer blows. There was less tension in the air and much more continuity in Curtis' play. Our dialogues flowed easier and he more readily shared his ups and downs in the classroom. He is learning to settle his problems with others without getting into fistfights; there is less anxiety and tension in his voice when he describes his battles in the school.

MARCH 6

Today Curtis finished a picture he was making for his mother. He was having a good day and our hour flowed smoothly with no major issues between us. I felt really good about seeing him so alive, whole, happy, and smiling. It was a joyous hour!

MARCH 13

Our hour was dampened by a late start due to a transportation problem. Both of us were disappointed in the delay; I was feeling sluggish and rather low-keyed. Curtis, too, was quieter than usual. It took longer today for us to become absorbed in each other. I was aware of my own responsibility for this. Curtis was disappointed that we would not see each other next week. In the last few minutes he attacked me verbally, saying he would kill me if he missed any of three darts he was about to throw. I told him I did not like that and thought it was unfair. He lessened his threat as I repeated my refusal to accept his condition. Unfortunately, our shortened session was over before we could resolve the conflict. I wondered what had created the anger after last week's joyous meeting—his unhappiness over our short session, the news of no session on the 20th, or was he reacting to my low-keyed mood? I struggled with myself but did not feel I touched the source.

[cereta perry]

THE TEACHER FOR
HUMANISTIC EDUCATION

MANY STUDENTS COME to Merrill-Palmer searching for ways to enrich life for themselves and others. Those who join us in the program "Enhancing Human Potentials in Young Children and Their Families" commit themselves to work with children, teachers, and community people in creating exciting and alive learning climates. Students arrive with an awareness of the destructive consequences of traditional education; they have often had direct experience with authoritarian administrators and teachers. They know what it is like to be in a classroom of narrow academic objectives that are being pursued without the slightest regard for learners' goals. They have frequently witnessed spontaneity and individual expression being suppressed, while repetitive, imitative behavior was being encouraged.

Although students recognize what is required to live humanly, many bring with them prejudices about black children, as revealed in the following conceptions:

1. Black children live in environments which are devoid of essential early experiences needed to prepare them for excellence in school, appropriate sex-role behavior, and effective participation in life generally. Because of these limiting factors, black children are culturally deprived.

2. Since black children come from lower-class backgrounds, they must be impulsive and immature, and have less tolerance for stress than their white peer group.

3. Black children have low self-esteem and, therefore, poor self-concepts.

4. The homes of black children are weak in intellectual and moral content, and are generally chaotic places in which to grow.

5. Because black children are so different, it is necessary to learn special ways of relating to them.

As white students struggle to eradicate these distortions, they disclose the psychological distance between themselves and black people. A psychologist on the staff of the National Institute of Mental Health, as quoted by Kenneth B. Clark, made the following statement, which characterizes the predicament of many of our students.

The awesome shame and guilt that might otherwise overwhelm millions of fair-minded and well-meaning whites in both North and South is held in check by ignorance of the shocking facts or assuaged by pernicious rationalizations. It is comforting, self-absolving, to believe that the Negro's innate shortcomings are responsible for his present condition, and hard to acknowledge that the circumstances we force him to live under may be the very cause of this condition.

Another fundamental that must be grasped is the magnitude of the present psychological gulf between whites and non-whites. The growing anger of the more vocal Negroes, fanned and fed by a growing impatience, comes as a surprise to whites who live comfortably and peacefully far removed from the major Negro centers. The Negro and his problems never impinge on their thinking, their world, their smooth-running democracy. For them "sit-ins" and "still-ins" and "freedom rides" are evidence of irresponsibility, of unreasonableness, of lawlessness, or radicalism that reinforce all the myths they have learned to believe. On the other hand, when such whites do come face to face with the Negro world they discover in themselves an entirely new response: fear. They sense the Negro's envy of the "privileged caste," they sense some of his bitterness. They see sometimes the flaring anger that injustice breeds. They realize for the first time how far most Negroes have been forced into a world apart, a world so unfamiliar to the average white person that it could as well be in a foreign land. And in this alien world they discover a complement to the white man's rejection: the Negro's distrust. For the failure of the white man thus far to deal honestly and fairly with his non-white fellow citizens has bred a suspicion so deep that very few whites are ever trusted. And out of this recognition of distrust springs an unreasoned, and often unacknowledged fear.[1]

As the student becomes aware of his fear, he recognizes it as a significant barrier in all of his interactions with non-whites. He needs to confront himself regarding his position on black-white relationships. Through direct contact with black people he experiences something of the real world from which they come, and learns who they are as individual persons.

To counteract distortions and prejudices we offer students a wide range of direct and varied contacts with black children in one-to-one relations, in small groups, and in large groups. We also afford involvement with teachers, parents, and community leaders. Through these contacts students learn what is important in black communities, the tremendous range in child-rearing practices, the varying degrees of positive self-concepts in children, and the variety of aspirations parents have for their children. They come to know black people as individuals. It then becomes clear that black people, like other human beings, want an environment rooted in human values, both in the neighborhood and in the school.

As students become involved through dialogue and direct experience, they realize that current educational environments must change if education is to be a vital human experience; and that they themselves must change if they are to become effective leaders of humanistic education.

---

[1] Kenneth B. Clark, *Dark Ghetto* (New York: Harper & Row, Publishers, Inc., 1965), pp. 224–25. Reprinted by permission of Harper & Row, Publishers, Inc., and Victor Gollancz Ltd.

Change introduces the idea of innovation. As innovation has become a byword in education, traditional curricular offerings and classroom practices have become threatened. The threat uncovers many inadequate and frustrating relationships existing between teachers and learners and discloses that little has been done to help teachers develop effective interpersonal relationships.

Observation in many classrooms identifies the teacher's use of suggestion, command, and disapproval as regular tools to influence the learner's behavior. Sometimes these methods are successful; the fact that they are enables the teacher to label the resistant learner a "problem," or a "difficult child." It is true that such a child does create a problem for the teacher, but if the teacher understood what motivated the child's resistance, then the preferences and interests of the child might become valued factors in learning.

In order to foster humanistic education, the teacher must recognize both the affective and cognitive components of learning. The teacher who is willing and able to use his self in positive ways becomes involved in the stimulation and facilitation of growth in learners. Understanding and acceptance of self are important requirements for the teacher who wishes to help children reach their maximum in human growth and development. If the teacher is not involved in self-understanding, he will continue to see students through the biases and distortions of his own unrecognized needs, fears, anxieties, and hostile impulses.

When students enroll in our program, they make a commitment to deal forthrightly with the changes necessary in themselves and to become totally involved in the process required to bring about changes in educational environments. At some point, early in the dialogue, each student ponders the following significant questions:

Can I make an honest appraisal of the degree to which I am able to contribute to a fruitful learning climate?

Do I really want to make changes in me and my current practices?

Am I willing to experience the pain and work involved in total commitment to change?

In turn, Clark and I as faculty members of the program unit

make a commitment to each student to meet with the person, remain in personal, in-depth communication, offer resources and consultation, struggle with issues and problems that arise, and in every way participate actively in facilitating individual growth and developing important relationships. We are also fully committed to the children, teachers, administration, and community people with whom we work in initiating and developing a process of relevant and honest communication, a human learning climate, and an openness, freedom, and awareness in the schools. Thus, we offer students not total license to venture freely in any direction, at any time, with whomever they wish, but rather a definite structure in and through which there are expanded opportunities for preference, choice, interest, idiosyncratic behavior, unique creations, and, in general, almost limitless variations on our basic themes. The structure we offer includes seminars, workshops and practicum, a specific population of primary-age children, teachers, administrators, and community people, and a definite setting—the public school in poverty areas of Detroit. We believe the structure and direction provide substance and depth in and through which unique contributions can be made. Thus, our project is not for everyone, but is meant for persons who also want to commit themselves to human life in the classroom and are willing to tap fully their own energies and resources to bring about real growth in themselves and others.

A program of specific experiences is offered the student to facilitate his journey and enable him to discover more effective ways of being. Specifically, the program includes seminars in personal growth, psychological counseling, issues and problems in enhancing human potentials, an interpersonal-process experience, practicum work, and weekly individual supervisory conferences.

PERSONAL GROWTH AND PSYCHOLOGICAL COUNSELING

Personal Growth and Psychological Counseling is a didactic seminar focusing on an exploration of self, human values, and significant interpersonal experience, in the context of therapeutic relationships with children and adults. Concepts, principles, and styles reflected in the interpersonal process are presented and discussed. The place of emotions, dialogue, mystery, and intuition are explored; essential conditions in the therapeutic relationship are examined.

Being aware of students in the beginning and remaining open to them in their year-long journey, we include three general areas in the organization of the seminar. From the vast arena of psychological-educational content, the following themes have emerged as most essential:

A. *Self-Exploration*

The significance of individuality

Self-actualization

Myths related to mental illness

Authenticity

Honesty

Responsibility

Creativity

Confrontation

Self-enhancement through movement, music, drama, and art

Issues and problems

B. *Classroom Activities*

Relationships, awareness, and communication in children's literature

Human approaches to reading, science, and mathematics

Role-playing and dramatics as an integral part of the primary curriculum

Building relationships in the classroom

Issues and problems

C. *Therapy with Children*

Therapy: process, significance of focusing, encounters, essential conditions, unique and unpredictable dimensions

Setting and holding limits

Resources needed to set up the playroom
Issues and problems

From the many significant experiences afforded students during this seminar I have selected two to present in some detail.

ART EXPERIENCE AS A WAY OF SELF-ENHANCEMENT

I approach this experience with excitement and enthusiasm as I recognize it as a truly vital avenue for self-expression and self-enhancement. Students immediately see the potential of this activity to move them along on the continuous journey of self-growth.

Several small groups of three students each informally sit in a large room and become involved in a discussion focused on the significance of color in their lives. Observation of the groups reveals animated, personal interaction among the three persons in each group, as they explore:

a. the significance of color for me;
b. my ability to express myself through color;
c. the degree to which I use color as a means of communication.

After fifteen minutes of discussion, I invite the students to experience a variety of colors through the use of soft pastels and paper. However, the first involvement with colors is often influenced by the silence or sounds of the room and by the sounds outside. Each student has a tray of pastels (eight colors) and is encouraged to be leisurely in getting acquainted with the colors on his tray. He is then asked to select the color that he likes least and to express that feeling of "least liking" on paper. Following this, he selects the color that he likes best and expresses the feeling of "best liking" on paper. Then comes the experience of integrating the least-liked and best-liked colors in one unified expression.

The next activity in the art project is that of getting in touch with each of several feelings and expressing these feelings through the pastels. Those suggested are serenity, anger, fear, loneliness, and joy. Each student appears introspective as he gets in touch with these feelings and expresses them on paper.

When students are putting feelings of anger on paper, there is more sound and more expressive body language than at any other time during the preliminary work with colors. Recently, I observed one student working with such intensity that contact of the chalk with the paper tore the paper into small pieces.

When the "feeling" expressions have been completed, the student selects one of his creations and joins his group of three to share verbally the nature of the experience. The opportunity to share adds meaning to the experience and brings the group into more intimate contact.

Music is next added to the experience of color. A different recording is used to accompany each expression. The student is asked to portray the following through colors: (a) his body, (b) himself as a child, (c) himself as a teenager, and (d) himself as he is now. For the final experience of "colors with music" the student is invited to join the two other people in his group and create something new. Often a student begins to work in a small corner of the paper and gradually moves into the area of the two others in the group. One student felt so threatened when another began working prematurely in his area that he stopped working except for making superficial markings. In another instance, the three simultaneously rejected a drawing when they became aware that they were working independently instead of cooperatively. They then created a piece jointly.

The third component of the art experience is movement. An activity is created that challenges the student to unify colors with music and movement. As a recording is played, the student, while lying on the floor, moves around, always keeping as much body surface as possible in touch with the floor. At the conclusion of the record, the student puts these feelings to paper.

Next, the student stands and moves any part or parts of his

body except his feet. The feeling of this experience is put to paper.

Finally the student is free to move around the entire room. Following this experience of spontaneous movement, the total group works in a cooperative venture expressing their feelings through pastels.

Students regard the art experience as exhilarating. In the process they feel that they gain significant data about themselves. As they continue to learn about themselves as persons and to value their uniqueness, they are able to recognize and enjoy the individuality of each child with whom they work and to experience the child as a person and as a human being of immeasurable worth.

CREATING AN IDENTITY POSTER

It is unfortunate that words cannot transmit the depth of feeling generated by students as they create and share their identity posters. The identity poster is an expression of the vital experiences which characterize and differentiate the person in his formative and growing years and in the present. The following comments are made to introduce and pave the way to a serious commitment:

1. Present something of marked significance with reference to yourself as a child, as a teen-ager, and in the present. You may express these peak and depth moments through a poem, a drawing, an object, a paragraph.

2. Present data in your own way about the person or persons who helped you most to find your identity.

3. What was the greatest obstacle you had to overcome to achieve your sense of identity?

4. What are your hopes for the Merrill-Palmer experience?

5. Do not reveal your name but if you have a name which you would have chosen for yourself, give yourself this name.

The posters are created in absolute privacy and are hung in our seminar room in privacy. Each time a new poster is added, it is as

if a town crier went out shouting, "A new poster is up!" A number
of Merrill-Palmer students (not enrolled in our program unit) come
to the seminar room to study the posters and attempt to identify the
creator. At the end of the year each student shares the feelings he
experienced during the creation of the poster. Personal responses of
students clearly convey the value of the experience in getting to
know and accept themselves and others, and as a significant venture
in being known and in coming to know others.

SEMINAR IN ISSUES AND PROBLEMS

The seminar in issues and problems is the result of students' requests for a definite time to deal with problems related to the practicum experience. The content of the seminar is open-ended to allow for response to immediate or current needs expressed by students. As students work in the school, initiating activities and projects
designed to help children discover and develop their potentials, issues and problems arise which are resolved through group discussion and action.

The most outstanding issues have been (1) the reduction of
students' anxiety regarding participation in classroom programs; (2)
enrichment of teacher-student meetings; (3) organization and administration of the play-therapy program, and (4) dissemination of
knowledge gained from the practicum. When students spend time
observing in classrooms to become familiar with the teacher, the
children, and the learning climate, they become increasingly anxious
as they wonder what the experience will be for them as active participants. They become keenly aware that reading about humanistic
projects in formal education situations is different from the actual
initiation of such projects. They would feel better if there could
be some kind of "trial run." To meet this student request, we find
it helpful to make available video tapes of the work of our former
students as they initiated creative projects in classrooms; we also
set up "work sessions" so that students actually experience classroom
activities; and we encourage students to become familiar with the

materials (records, film strips, puppets, story tapes, etc.) in our resource room.

THE INTERPERSONAL-PROCESS SEMINAR

The interpersonal-process seminar is a significant resource in creating an active community of twelve people. In October, a group of ten students, strangers to each other and to Clark and me, assemble for our first seminar meeting. The group meets twice a month for two-and-a-half to three hours each session during the entire academic year. As the group meets, the struggles center on the development of authentic relationships, the honest expression of a wide range of emotional responses, an understanding of one's impact on one other person and on a group, the development of a greater awareness of one's own needs and the needs of others, and learning to communicate with honesty and directness. The spirit of community which develops amidst the group enables each individual to extend himself beyond the group and to approach others with real care and concern, indicating a valuing of the dignity of each person he encounters.

I have selected written expressions from several students in the community to provide the reader with some understanding of the students' feelings regarding the interpersonal-process seminar.

I.

I think the first deeply personal struggle for me was not only getting in touch with my feelings of the moment but also learning how to express them. Instead of fighting to hold them inside, I had to change tactics, to get them outside so that others could have someone to react and respond to. My greatest problem was not with the joyful feelings, but with the sad and lonely feelings. Sad, lonely, confused feelings are hard for an independent person like me to share or even release with others.

The next important struggle was that of confrontation. Here

I had defeated myself for a long time by thinking a confrontation would hurt another. As I struggled with the notion of confronting a member of the group, I soon felt great pain within my body. The only way for me to get relief was to confront the person with whom I had an issue. The experience was extremely painful and unpleasant, but so freeing that there can be no turning back.

The entire experience of the development of individuals through group interaction was strange to me. With group support, especially the support of the leaders, I have tried to take the many, seemingly endless risks on the path to authenticity.

II.

My biggest struggle was to become actively, vocally involved in the meetings. Though attentive and focused, I was passive. I went through several stages. At first I was comfortable with my silence; then I felt guilty about it, and finally I felt okay about it. This is me: it is all right to be silent. Then I gradually became more vocal and the interactions I had in the meetings, though few in number, were important. One of my most significant interactions was my confrontation of a group member with my feelings of anger. I felt angry because I experienced her being critical of my efforts. The result of the confrontation was a clarification of my relationship with my colleague. It changed from an ignoring of each other to a relationship in which there were positive interchanges, and then cooperative efforts took place between us. Another plus for me resulting from the confrontation was a realization of how I (used to) let what I thought others were thinking about me influence my behavior. I learned from this experience to check it out with the speaker.

III.

My ongoing struggle of this year has been judgment vs. acceptance. The more I have been able to accept myself, my feelings in the present, the more I feel accepting of others. I feel that my need to judge myself and others was a great weight that had me pinned down and unable to move. I feel very happy about my growth toward acceptance.

Through the struggles, the confrontations, the silences, the affirmations, the real caring of one person for another, a joyous exciting community comes to be. At one point, about two-thirds of the way along our recently completed year, the group began to experience the excitement and closeness of being and working together. These students created activities beyond work and study which provided additional opportunities to share life together. At the end of the year we went off on an extended camp-out and freely enjoyed each other in music, song, nature walks, spontaneous dialogues, and resolution of unfinished business. It was a beautiful union of individuality and community which the interpersonal-process seminar had helped to create.

THE SUPERVISORY CONFERENCE

We find that, in addition to the seminars, the supervisory conference provides an important source of support for the student as he accepts the challenge of commitment and as he explores a wider and deeper range of resources, activities, and relationships. Each student meets with us for one hour a week in a person-to-person relationship to explore issues and processes related to his work in the school, his play-therapy sessions, his seminars, and his own growth. We are also available in moments of emergency or crisis.

Because we view supervision as a facilitative process and we value the self-motivating attitude, we encourage the student to come to the conference inclined to explore the concerns of his choice and to seek whatever support or guidance he needs to execute the responsibilities of his commitment.

We find during the course of the year that students focus on the following concerns:

1. Need for support and encouragement in areas which are new and personally significant.

2. Development of sufficient trust in and valuing of oneself so that the student will not become victimized by external situations.

3. Involvement in a process of self-growth and a development of comfortable feelings in being oneself and in accepting ambiguities in life and work.

4. Creation of a healthy balance of feeling, sensing, and knowing as the student develops resources and actualizes his potential for learning and living.

5. Permitting one's self and the self of others to be.

6. Learning to identify the real issues so that decision and action are central rather than peripheral.

7. Learning to recognize barriers, both internal and external, that interfere with communication and that are sometimes aroused by current challenges and sometimes a carry-over from past relationships.

The climate of the supervisory conference, and the nature of the one-to-one relationship, provide the student with freedom and trust in plunging into his personal concerns at a deep level. He often gains the strength in the supervisory conference to reveal his problems in the interpersonal-process seminar and to face issues and challenges in work and in relations with others.

THE PRACTICUM

The practicum is the experience which affords our students direct contact with children, teachers, administrators, and parents. It offers several opportunities for students: (a) to initiate activities and projects designed to humanize learning and to promote the creative process in school; (b) to promote experiences in play therapy for children who indicate the need for a special relationship; and (c) to participate in adult community groups to learn how these groups, through joint action, effect changes in the school.

DIRECT INVOLVEMENT IN THE CLASSROOM

In order to promote creative processes in the classroom, the student is assigned to work with one or more teachers and paraprofessionals.

The school staff and the Merrill-Palmer student work as a team, initiating, planning, and developing projects designed to help children discover and use their potentials. In addition to planning time with teachers, the student participates in classrooms two to four mornings a week, actively involved with children in a facilitating way. As children are introduced to various projects in the arts and sciences, the facilitating team is available to help as needed. (Some of the projects are discussed in the chapter "Encounters in Learning.")

PLAY THERAPY

Our students participate in decisions regarding children who come to Merrill-Palmer for play therapy. When the teacher or student recognizes a child who needs a special relationship in play therapy, they discuss the behavior which indicates this. The child is then brought to the attention of the school counselor, who makes the referral to us and completes the administrative detail. The student is assigned as therapist to children from classrooms other than the one in which he works.

From the moment the student and the child enter the playroom, they are involved in the development of a creative relationship. The students struggle to internalize authentically the creative relationship as developed by Moustakas in *Psychotherapy With Children:*

> When two persons meet in a creative relationship, there is a continuing sense of mutuality and togetherness throughout the experience. Therapist and children are involved in a process of self-fulfillment, a growth experience which has a wholly positive orientation and direction. There is constancy and consistency of self within which new patterns, images and configurations appear. Together, therapist and child create unique themes of life, whether it be in the realm of deep mutual silence, in their dramas of important personal figures, or in their fresh expressions. Such a relationship cannot be understood by studying the behavior of the adult and the child. Behavior in the creative relationship is only an external fragment

of the total experience. It includes, in addition to the unique individuals, certain transcendental qualities which connect these two persons with all of human life and human welfare.

The whole idea of errors or mistakes in the creative relationship is irrelevant. It is not possible to do right or wrong in such a relationship. It is a matter of being, of presence, of thisness, of a life being lived rather than a matter of individuals acting and being acted upon. All references to responses and their correctness or incorrectness are inappropriate. These are judgments valid to a reactive situation where definite goals exist and where the therapist's behavior can be rated in terms of its contribution to the realization of these goals.

In the creative relationship, changes do occur. It is inevitable that when individuals really meet as persons and live together they learn in suffering, frustration, and despair as well as in joy and fulfillment. It is my contention, however, that the creative relationship does not address itself to motivation, learning, and change but only to the interests, capacities, and ways of two persons. The reality of the creative relationship in therapy cannot be understood on the basis of the changes which occur. The changes are not the basic process of the relationship; not even a goal or focus of the relationship. Attempting to understand the creative relationship on the basis of motivation, strategy, goals and outcomes is futile. Such terms are meaningless. They relate to outside-of-life situations and can be used to understand about, or learn about, or study about something discrete, static and nonexistential. The creative relationship can be considered only through denotation or utterance, or through pointing to it, and can be known only through living it! It is my belief that such a relationship cannot be brought about no matter how fervently the therapist may desire it or how rich his background of experience in such relationships. The creative relationship happens. But once it occurs, the therapist can decide to participate in it as a matter of choice.[2]

The problems emerging from the play-therapy program result from the total involvement of our students. They are classroom facilitators, drivers for the children who come to Merrill-Palmer for therapy, receptionists for the children and child therapists. It is

[2] Clark Moustakas, *Psychotherapy With Children* (New York: Harper and Row, Publishers, 1959), pp. 135–36.

desirable that the student serving as therapist for a child relate to the child in that capacity only. This fact alone creates real scheduling problems. Since during the year some children terminate the experience while others are beginning, additional problems arise. Group discussion and action are invaluable in resolving these problems.

Our students encounter struggles as they become involved in the development of the creative relationship. Some of the issues with which they struggle again and again are (1) the idea that there is a right way and a wrong way to be in the playroom; (2) the response to the child's behavior instead of to the child's feelings; (3) the child's silence; (4) the matter of setting and maintaining limits, and (5) the appropriateness of sharing one's own feelings with the child.

An excerpt from a student's report of a child in therapy is included here to present the struggle as one student experienced it.

> Jim played with Bobo and began to let the air out. He turned to me to ask if it would be okay to let the air out and not blow it up again. I told him he could do what he wanted to do. He responded, "Yeah, but I know what *you really want!*"
>
> I guess I really didn't want him to let the air out but didn't have the courage to say so to him.
>
> The next time Jim came in, he went immediately to Bobo and asked permission to let the air out. This time I said "No" (I had discussed my concern in a supervisory conference). His immediate response was, "How come you let me do it last time?" I said I hadn't really wanted to then. He said he knew it; he had doubted me when I said it was okay. He accepted the "No" and without further discussion went on with his play.

A fuller development of the struggles our students encounter is reported in the chapter "The Play-Therapy Program."

SCHOOL AND COMMUNITY PARTICIPATION

The Williams School Neighborhood Committee and the Williams School Community Council provide students with opportunities to experience community action regarding the school's program. Students attend monthly meetings of the Williams School Neighborhood Committee to learn the specific activities through which the community is supporting and enriching the program of the school. Further, the School Community Council, with the assistance of Merrill-Palmer, organizes group experiences designed to develop effective communication between school personnel and community residents. Our students participate in leading these groups.

The bimonthly meetings of the Williams School teachers and the Merrill-Palmer students and staff are important in establishing and maintaining positive relationships. It is during these meetings that all persons connected with the program assemble to share experiences and get to know one another. These meetings are constantly reassessed in order to create an alive and moving spirit among all.

During the year numerous requests and opportunities arise to share with various school and community populations our experiences at the Williams School. Our students accept the responsibility for creating and presenting programs that will vividly present the values, methods, and results of our efforts to humanize learning in primary-unit classrooms.

CONCLUDING OBSERVATIONS

Having experienced the arduous task of self-exploration, followed by changes in their own perceptions of self, our students are more able to be copartners with teachers in humanizing learning in public-school classrooms.

It is remarkable to observe the ways in which the experienced classroom teacher is willing to enter into the spirit of the journey when the student is open, accepting, valuing.

As our students come to recognize their own potential, they are able to realize that all children have untapped reservoirs of potential, that all children can learn with meaning and value. Our students are eager to be effective in releasing this potential and in discovering the most direct path to creative achievement. Their work with children in classrooms reveals success in this area. The group of teachers recently involved expressed the desire to have our students remain a second year.

The belief that one needs to learn a special way of relating to black children is radically altered as our students respond to the human qualities of each child and relate in free and natural ways. Our students learn, too, that when they respond to the strengths of children the prejudicial trappings are irrelevant. Life in the classroom comes to be exciting and growth-promoting whether in art, music, literature, movement, science, reading, or math. What matters are the unique persons involved and the human presentation of resources, materials, and activities.

It is clear that our students grow to regard children as more important than skills or subject matter; all content and material become avenues through which children develop their own resources.

From numerous possibilities and alternatives, children are encouraged to make decisions about what and how they want to learn. The entire area of interpersonal relationships is enlarged. Since the focus is on learning instead of teaching, the distance between teacher and learner is greatly reduced and in time open, strong relations develop.

As an advocate for creating an effective learning climate in public schools, I am most encouraged after my experience with the Merrill-Palmer students in the program unit "Enhancing Human Potentials in Young Children and Their Families." Students are able to respond to the affective components of learning and integrate them with the cognitive components. These values facilitate operation of a truly human classroom in which joy and excitement accompany every facet of the learning process and children come to be alive and free.

[clark moustakas]

OPEN-COMMUNICATION GROUPS
Joining of Community People and School Staff

WHEN WE FIRST BECAME INVOLVED with parents, teachers, and administrators in our efforts to humanize learning in the primary grades, Cereta and I envisioned as part of our program the setting up of workshops and small group sessions that would facilitate communication and establish free and open relations between community people and school staff. Although a workshop was conducted the summer before we entered the school to begin our project, and although we had the support of both neighborhood and school people, we were a long way from organizing communication groups. An entire year was to pass before we were invited to become members of the Strategy Committee representing the Community Council of the school, an action group of community representatives and school staff empowered to make decisions in regard to hiring and firing, the procurement of materials and equipment, and determining curriculum priorities. It was an indication of community acceptance and trust when we became voting members of the committee. As a result of the efforts of the Strategy Committee, numerous neighborhood projects were designed which included evening classes for parents in science, math, and reading; a film program; Red Cross training, and numerous social functions such as parent lunch days, coffee hours, and potluck suppers. An especially exciting project involved community people "teaching" classes for children utilizing their own skills in carpentry, cooking, sewing, electronics, mechanics, and other areas. These classes were to begin with demonstrations and would be followed by more regular, continuing sessions for children interested in learning and applying the skills involved. The aim was to bring into the school unemployed and retired persons in the community who were interested in sharing their skills with children. These people would be paid as special consultants. A fourth project was called Open-Discussion Groups— a name devised by the president of the Community Council, Mrs. Thomas, who had stated that honest communication was lacking between community and school people, that community people did not feel comfortable and welcome in the school, and that teachers were not comfortable visiting the homes of parents. She proposed the forming of open-discussion groups made up of community people, teachers, paraprofessionals, and administrators. The response was immediate, supportive, affirmative. Cereta and I practically leaped with joy, since we felt that this type of group involvement was necessary to unify community and school efforts. We had suggested it when we first began our work but at that time we were met with fear and silence. Now the entire Strategy Committee was not only in favor, but was anxious to begin. The committee organized six open-discussion groups, consisting of an equal number of community and school people. The groups were formed with the assistance of Mr. Isom, the school principal, and Mrs. Thomas. All of the projects of the Strategy Committee were open to all teachers, paraprofessionals and community people—not just those involved with primary-unit children.

Our first group contained five community people and five school people. Cereta and I were asked to serve as coleaders and two of our graduate students joined us as trainees, with the understanding that they would later cooperate in leading their own groups. Each group was to meet for three sessions of two hours each. But, as with other plans, this was changed following our first group meeting, which extended forty minutes beyond the time limit. Then Mrs. Carson (a neighborhood person), somewhat upset about stopping, announced that she wished we could go on. "Can't we have an open-ended session?" she pleaded. "We need a natural stopping place. When we're ready, we stop." The group agreed to make the last meeting an open-ended session. "Great!" shouted Mrs. Shore. "I'll bring my sleeping bag."

I made a few remarks to open the meeting, mostly to create an atmosphere of relaxation but also to point to a direction. I indicated that the group meetings were strictly to deal with communication barriers in relationships, and not with school projects or school goals. I then asked if anyone was ready to open up an issue with another person. Practically before I had the words out, Mrs. Thomas jumped in and lunged forward in the direction of Mr. Isom. The essence of her communication was that he didn't pay much attention to her, didn't think he had to cooperate with her, and did nothing on his own as a follow-through to her suggestions. She expressed her disgust in strong language, averting her body and almost never looking at him directly. Mr. Isom responded, in his usual slow and gentle way, "As far as I know I've cooperated with you in every way." This remark seemed to increase her antagonism, as Mrs. Thomas shouted with intense feeling, "I don't get nothing from you. It's like talking to a blank wall. I do all the work and all the thinking. I ask you to get some jobs done and I don't know what you're thinking." Mr. Isom, tightened in body, turned directly toward Mrs. Thomas. Without a change in the level or tone of his voice, he answered, "Mrs. Thomas, if you would be more specific I could comment more accurately. If you mean the ten thousand dollars we have to spend by the end of April, I've been telling you for weeks there's no way we can spend that money on training of community people to be more effective leaders or more effective parents by April 30—and we desperately need the list of equipment items I gave you."

"No! That's not what I'm talking about," she shouted. "Just the other day I asked you to send out notices to community people to call a meeting to approve our budget for training and implementation of our program. You just stood there dumbfounded. I had no way of knowing what you were thinking."

With some anger in his voice, Mr. Isom responded: "To tell you the truth I was dumbfounded. You came into my office and asked me to call a meeting on a one-day notice. Who do you think will come? You've got to give people more time than that. Even though I didn't like it, I went ahead and had your announcement mimeographed and sent out. Then, when we don't get much of a response (with more anger in his voice), you point the finger at me."

At this juncture several parents and teachers broke in, generally supporting Mr. Isom's observations. Mrs. Thomas stiffened and during the next ten minutes, with the strong anger in her voice, let the group know that in addition to her work as president of the council, she had a husband and two children to care for, and a full-time job. "I'm tired, just tired, of having to explain to everyone and having to repeat everything everywhere I go, having to call everyone and remind them of meetings, having to write notices and reports."

Mr. Isom interrupts: "My main objection to you is that you don't give me time to think things out, to plan with you. You expect me to jump up and rush to carry out your suggestions."

"Not my suggestions, Mr. Isom. *Council's* suggestions. You refer to the body, not to me as an individual."

"Okay but the point is I need more time to carry out these plans. I have my own staff to discuss these projects with and get support."

"Mrs. Thomas," I ask, "are you feeling, too, that Mr. Isom doesn't respect you? That when he is silent you feel he is disapproving and doesn't have a regard for you as a person?"

"Yes, I do feel that."

Mr. Isom interrupts: "Mrs. Thomas, if I didn't respect you I wouldn't do the things you ask. I'm only asking that you give me more time to act, and more time to prepare my staff. I hope you can understand my position, too."

A period of silence followed, and then Mrs. Carson (a member of the community council) spoke (literally shouting): "If you two want to rest awhile, I have something I'll throw on the table.

"Mrs. Thomas, to be perfectly honest, I feel with you the way you feel with Mr. Isom. You come into the school nearly every day. You hardly ever ask my opinion about council plans. You come right into the office where I'm working and you don't never say nothing to me. You talk all the time to Mr. Marvine and get his opinions, but it's like I'm not even there. You got yourself way up there and I'm way down here. You talk only to the big shots. It didn't used to be that way. Remember when we worked together and took trips together? We could laugh and carry on, but ever since you became chairman of the council you act high and mighty."

"If Mr. Marvine wants your opinion, he can ask you. I'm not going to talk to every individual in the school. That's not my job. Don't be like that with me. I don't have time. I be rushing around getting babysitters for my children, cooking meals in advance. I . . . uh . . ."

"Mrs. Thomas, that's not what I'm talking about. I'm busy, too, but I could help if you'd let me. I could take some of the burden."

"I already have four officers and I have to push them. I don't need no more executives."

"Wait a minute, Mrs. Thomas," Mr. Watts shouts, "you never give us a chance to do things. Besides, we work out an agenda for a meeting and then you come in and wipe it away and say we gotta discuss somethin' else."

"Mr. Watts, hold your fire. I'm not through saying what I gotta say to Mrs. Thomas and I wanta get it all out. Mrs. Thomas, you and I used to be friends, but since you got this job you don't have time for me. You only share with Mrs. Jones—just the two of you working everything out."

"Mrs. Thomas," I comment, "the way you've turned your body away from Mrs. Carson, you must be feeling very angry right now."

"Mrs. Carson understands me. Black people know how to talk with black people. They understand each other."

"Mrs. Thomas," Cereta shouts, "what are you saying? You know from your own experience today that's not true. And the other day at our strategy meeting Mrs. Jones said her daughter was skating in school. I didn't know what she was talking about but Clark understood her. You remember that!"

Mrs. Ames (a paraprofessional) comes into the discussion:

"Mrs. Thomas, every one of us is an individual whether we're black or not, and we understand when we listen and hear not just because we're black but because of who we are."

"You and I aren't understanding each other right now, Mrs. Thomas," shouts Mrs. Carson. "We still got our defenses up."

"Well, I can tell you all. Right now, I'm tired. I'm very tired, attending all these meetings, rushing one place and another, people calling me all hours to find out what's going on. I thought when we broke up into small committees each one would do the job, but they don't do nothing. I gotta go do everything to see that the work is done. I'm tired. If this is the way it's gotta be, I tell you right now I'm quitting."

Mr. Watts, speaking to Mrs. Thomas: "I asked to help. I told you I'd drive you anytime anywhere you wanta go even if I have to change my work hours."

Mrs. Carson, shouting again: "That's not why I brought this up. These feelings been burdening me so I haven't been sleeping nights thinking about you. I didn't sleep last night worrying about how I was going to let you know. I just wanta know you respect me. I wanta help you do your job. I work at the school every day. I see community people. I'd take your notices right to every home. I could if you'd ask me."

"The council has its own way of doing jobs," answers Mrs. Thomas. "I don't like the way you speak."

Cereta, speaking especially to Mrs. Thomas: "Mrs. Thomas, you're the one who asked for these open-communication groups. Remember, you're the person who said it was important for people to be honest if they were ever to relax and be free with each other. Well, Mrs. Carson is telling you how she feels when she's with you —small, unimportant, like she's almost not there. She's talking about you as a person and she's saying she doesn't like what's happening between you. She's not saying you're doing a poor job as chairman. She wants to be recognized and to become important in your life. Can't you respond to her feelings and not in terms of your job as president of the council?"

"I didn't know she was feeling neglected. Why didn't you tell me?"

"I wanted to but I didn't have the courage. Also, you present yourself as the body (representing the entire council) and not as an individual—just be Mrs. Thomas with me."

"When I bring a report it is the body, not me as an individual. Maybe I've been at this job long enough and it's time to quit."

"No, I wouldn't want that. You're doing a good job. Without you, we'd move slow. You do things in a hurry."

"Too much in a hurry for some people."

Mrs. Shore speaks to the entire group:

"Sometimes I worry when people talk to each other the way we have. We're all concerned about making life better for our children and we're not always aware of what the other person is doing. Here in this room, every one of us is stretching himself to provide opportunities for people to grow, but we each work in a different way. I'm very outgoing and bubbly and sometimes when I approach Mr. Isom in my wild way I think, 'He must think I'm some kind of nut.' He's so quiet and gentle, so reserved in everything—the way he talks, the way he walks, the way he works. But he's a beautiful man. No one works harder for our kids. And when I'm up against it, when I'm panicky, in an emergency I call on Mr. Isom. He just says 'Yes' and comes and in his calm manner he straightens out the mess. I have absolute confidence in him. Mrs. Thomas, it scares me when you talk about quitting. I see how much of your life you're putting into our school. No one can replace you now. Mrs. Carson and Mr. Watts don't want you to resign. We all know how much you've got to do and we're just hoping you'll spread the work out more, bring in more community people and let them take the burden off your shoulders."

This seemed like a good closing statement for our first session, and since we had already gone over our time limit I brought the meeting to a close. Mr. Hughes briefly expressed how much he valued Mrs. Thomas and Mr. Isom and pointed out that though they had very different styles they both had a way of getting their jobs done. Almost no one got up to leave. For almost two hours people continued their conversations in small groups.

In the interim between the first and second meetings, the

Strategy Committee met to determine the membership of the remaining five open-communication groups. People had been approached previously so that in the final arrangement each group included an equal number of community people and school staff. Several members of our first group asked if they could be stand-ins ready to replace any dropouts. Mr. Watts remarked that it was the most exciting group experience he'd ever had and that he was counting the days until the second meeting came. Cereta and I left with our hearts soaring—one of our earliest visions coming to fruition.

With heightened anticipation, the second session opened. Immediately, a series of exchanges took place, all revolving around anger, its value and limitations in relations. The parent group on the whole supported the view that angry expression was often necessary in clearing the air and paving the way for open communication. Mrs. Thomas remarked, "Anger doesn't turn people away. Not when you're honest and directly say what you gotta say." Referring to one of the teachers, she added, "The other day you was manipulating me. Just give it to me straight and I'll respond even if I don't agree with you." Several other parents commented along similar lines and indicated that they preferred to be leveled with rather than dealt with by an indirect approach. As the tensions between one of the teachers and several parents mounted, Mr. Isom became increasingly uncomfortable. "I think we overdid it," he said, "repeating again and again the same thing. I don't like it when we beat a dead horse. Tell a person once, twice, then let's move on. No point in hurting someone unnecessarily."

Cereta: "Mr. Isom, I object to that. No one here deliberately wants to hurt another person. I like Mrs. Simpson very much but I think she has difficulty handling anger. I think it is necessary to get all our feelings on the table. She got into the problem first with Mrs. Thomas but we're all trying to clarify our own relationship with Mrs. Simpson. Even when a person doesn't express anger directly, it comes out anyway and people are affected by it."

Mr. Watts: "We gotta be honest with each other—that's what these groups are for."

Mrs. Thomas: "Why, yes, I wasn't telling Mrs. Simpson to stop. It may sound funny but I liked it. (Turning to Mrs. Simpson): It was real when you talked on my level. I've always thought you were above me because you're a teacher and you're always proper. But that day you surprised me. I started looking at you in a different way. Though I backed off then, I think you're more human and I can approach you now."

Mrs. Shore enters the discussion.

"I think we should all keep in mind what these meetings are for—in the end to bring about a better world for our children."

Considerable discussion followed as to the purpose of the communication groups. Finally, it was clarified that Mrs. Shore was emphasizing that, if in the back of people's minds was the notion of helping children grow more fully, then parents and teachers could work together as an effective team. Each person would speak openly and honestly and face the tensions and issues involved, because ultimately this kind of direct open communication would lead to a true cooperation between school and community.

At this point the meeting came to a close, having extended half an hour beyond the scheduled time. For the next hour people remained and talked with each other in single relationships and in small groups.

The following week, before our marathon session began, Mr. Watts, in a spontaneous and exciting way, opened the meeting. Because of his previous silence, we were surprised when he plunged into a lengthy discussion of his childhood and youth. He then analyzed the process through which our group was evolving, gave his view of how individual members were developing their status in the group, and compared our group with the way a ghetto gang was established. It seemed that he had come primed and couldn't wait until we gathered to begin. I felt in him a desire to be recognized, to be heard as a strong voice. During the first two hours he engaged in dialogues with every person in the group. He described his battles to emerge as a person of power and respect, his fight to the top as a leader in his ghetto neighborhood. He pictured how he walked into a room and described the immediate response to his presence; his facial expression, he said, was enough to force a certain kind of action. Mrs. Carson seemed especially affected by his words since she grew up in the same neighborhood. She pointed her words sharply at Mr. Watts: "You're not telling it like it is—at least not for me."

"Mrs. Carson, you don't know what it's like for males in the ghetto. You don't see what happens behind the doors."

"Don't call it ghetto; it's our community; it's our neighborhood, not a ghetto."

"I don't care what you call it, Mrs. Carson. Stealing, lying, cheating, fighting—that was the way to move up. The law of the jungle ruled."

"My boys grew up in the same neighborhood!"

"You don't know what your boys do. My mamma woulda killed me if she knew the way I fought. You had to fight or you woulda been at the bottom all the time. It hasn't changed much either. People are robbed every day, attacked every day. Nobody believes in law and order. People looking right out the window seeing a robbery wouldn't report it. They know how to keep a lying face when the police are around. I been robbed three times. Everything. Wiped out. They threw all my stuff in the alley. I got it back one time but the last time I didn't."

"Report it to the police. I would, if I saw a robbery. We wouldn't let anyone rob our neighbors."

"Police don't do nothing. You gotta do it yourself. I know who robbed me but I got no proof. The neighbors clamp up. I gotta gun. I told the police I was gonna shoot the dude that did it. But they say I can't. They told me if I was there and actually saw him stealing I could shoot him dead. They say I *should* shoot him dead. And I know I would if I caught them in the act."

"Mr. Watts, that's no way to solve the problem."

"Mrs. Carson, it's the only way. Just like when we were kids. If they afraid of you, they respect you and don't steal from you no more."

Throughout this exchange, Mrs. Carson was growing increasingly agitated. Her knees began to shake. She got up, walked out of the room, and paced up and down the hallway. After about five minutes she returned and sat with her body turned away from Mr.

Watts. I asked her if she was angry with him. "Not angry," she answered, "upset. He don't tell it like it is for all of us. He should speak for himself. It's changing anyway. I'm block president and I know we're working together now to make our community a better place for our children. We don't have the alcohol and drugs and crimes the way it used to be."

"I tell you, Mrs. Carson, boys still fight it out to see who's going to be leader. The leader tells the others what to do and they do it. They respect the one that's strongest. They'll do what he tells them."

At this point, Mr. Hughes enters and he and Mr. Wilson discuss the difference between respect and fear. Mr. Hughes points out that the person you respect, you go all out for, but you only do the minimum for the one you fear. He concludes:

"That's why, Mr. Watts, in our school we want children to respect us for what we can offer them, not fear us because we hold a club over their heads. Reason—not muscle—and real talent—not phony display—are the basis for respect."

Since there was a pause at this point, I asked Mr. Watts if he would apply what he had been sharing to our group. He responded immediately.

"We don't use our fists here to solve our differences. We talk them over and settle them with the help of others."

"Do you think that would be a better way, even in your neighborhood?"

"Yes, but we don't have groups like these."

"Who is the leader in this group tonight?"

"I guess I am, since I'm directing the talking. In here, we're honest with each other. We tell people straight how we feel, but outside you gotta play a different role. You go around the block. You don't come honest right away and——"

Cereta interrupts: "Mr. Watts, Jim, you speak for yourself. I'm the same person wherever I am and it doesn't matter who I'm with. I don't go around the block. I tell the person directly what I think, how I feel."

"Dr. Perry, do you tell your boss you won't do something you don't believe in?"

"Yes I do, Jim. I certainly do."

"Well, Dr. Perry, I'm learning something tonight. I know we have to understand each other and be honest with each other to work together and help our children in the school. But on the outside I thought you gotta be polite and go around the block. I really learned something tonight. I'm gonna try it on you, Mr. Isom. Next time I got something to say to you that you may not like hearing, I'm coming into your office and tell you straight off."

Mr. Isom responds: "I'd like that, Mr. Watts, I really would."

Cereta comes in: "I would too, Jim. How come you bypassed me and told Mr. Isom you'd talk straight with him? You're avoiding me. Are you afraid of me?"

"No, Dr. Perry, but with you I think I better go around the block because if I say the wrong thing you may jump on me."

"Jim, I wouldn't jump on you, but if I'm angry I'll let you know."

"Dr. Perry, that's it. I don't want you to be angry at me."

"But my anger is only a way of straightening things out. Getting to the bottom of the trouble."

"Okay, Dr. Cereta, from now on I'll put it all out. If you don't like what I'm saying, that's your problem. I've really learned something tonight. Honesty is a better way to communicate and work together than going around the block. I'm going to be practicing that. This group is helping me not only to be relaxed and free here but to try out some of these ideas outside."

Almost before Mr. Watts's last words are out, Mrs. Carson speaks to Mr. Isom.

"Mr. Isom, I have that feeling with you, too. Sometimes when I'm supposed to give you a report I can't sleep at night. I lie awake all night going over and over in my mind how to talk with you. Then I come into your office and I'm all tongue-tied. I say a few words and run. I go and I give all my ideas to Mr. Marvine. I'm not supposed to do that. I should be able to talk directly to you."

"Yes, you really should. As a community person you'd be of great help to me."

"I wanted to tell you how you affected me the first night. You're way up high as principal and I'm just way down as a parent. I know you don't look at me that way."

"You know this community much better than I do, Mrs. Carson. Many times I need your guidance."

"I know that. Maybe now that I've told you, I'll be able to just come in natural and sit down and talk person-to-person without being nervous and uptight."

"I thought you preferred talking to Mr. Marvine, but now that I know, maybe I can help you be more comfortable when you come in. And I'll make more of a point of seeking you out."

After a short pause, I address Mr. Hughes, stating that in all three of the sessions his communications were reactions to others, that he had not at any time initiated something of his own that would help us to know him as a person. Mr. Hughes asks what I want to know, and I indicate I'd be interested in anything he wishes to share. There is no response. After an awkward silence, several other people in the group state that they have had the same experience with Mr. Hughes. Again, there is a long pause. I address Mr. Hughes once more.

"Bill, I notice you often initiate professional discussions. You can talk for hours about your teaching, your relations with children, the projects and field trips you're engaged in. But almost never have you shared what turns you on, what saddens you or fascinates you or excites you." Again, there is no response from Mr. Hughes. Cereta enters at this point.

"Bill, I see a pattern in your relations. On a professional basis you're terrific, but on a personal basis you leave all the responsibility to the other person. You take no initiative. I enjoy our work together but I wouldn't try establishing a friendship with you because I would have to do all the work."

Bill does not respond.

I then ask him: "Bill, do you want to continue?" No answer. I repeat the question. Again there is no answer.

Seeing what appears to be an expression of anger on his face, I ask him if he is angry at me for opening an area of conflict.

A long pause follows, which Mr. Watts interrupts: "You could cut it with a knife."

Another long pause. I address the group: "Since apparently Bill doesn't want to continue, perhaps someone else would move us on."

Paul: "But I'm concerned that you've approached Bill several times and he hasn't directly responded to you."

Bill: "I have nothing to say. I've heard what Cereta and Clark are saying and I need to think it through."

Mr. Watts: "Bill, that's your problem. You gotta think all the time instead of talking with your emotions. Don't think it over. Tell what you feel right away. Every time you stop, you leave us hanging. Say what you feel at the moment, not the next day."

"Okay, I felt angry at Clark before when he was pushing me, but I'm not angry now. I gotta know what he wants before I respond."

"It's not what I want but how you feel and who you are that matters."

"Okay, I hear you. I have to learn to be more spontaneous."

Short pause. "Well, if that's finished, I have an issue with someone," Mrs. Jones remarks, and she turns to face Mr. Isom.

"When I came in tonight, you gave me that look you always give me. So, I decided right away, he wants to know something I know and I'm not going to tell him. You never come right out and ask me. You play little games with me. If that's how you want to play, I'll play and win. I like to see you squirm. Just give you enough to keep you going."

"Mrs. Jones, when you came in I just moved over to offer you a seat and then——"

"Mr. Isom, I know better than that. I wasn't going to sit next to you. I saw your look so I came over here. You chased after me. I knew what you wanted but I decided to wait until you came right out and asked."

"Mrs. Jones, I already knew. Mr. Watts told me that, except for the trip, the entire proposal was approved."

"Then why were you bothering with me if you already knew?"

This type of communication continues for about fifteen minutes with neither of the persons giving ground. When it becomes repetitive, I interrupt.

"You're both saying the same things over again. You'd save a lot of time and energy if you expressed your feelings directly to each other. It's getting to be boring hearing you say things over and over."

Mrs. Jones cuts off my remark: "If he wants to go around the block, then I'll go around the block; when he stops I'll stop."

Cereta: "How come it always depends on Mr. Isom? Are you always going to do it his way? Are you always the follower? I'd think it would be more satisfying to give him a straight answer or a direct expression of your feeling."

Mrs. Jones: "No! Why should I? No strain for me. Don't take any energy to keep playing his game."

Mrs. Thomas: "Yes. They know what they're doing. They understand each other."

Clark: "Part of why we're here is to understand each other. But understanding alone is not enough. It doesn't mean anything at all if understanding doesn't lead to action. If people don't act on what they understand, it's just a lot of words. It's like playing the same record over and over again."

Mr. Watts: "If they're satisfied, that's all that matters."

Karen (one of our graduate students): "Mrs. Jones, I don't understand you at all. If you base your behavior on what the other person does, then you have no identity of your own. You're not a person at all."

Mrs. Jones: "I give them what they want. If they play a game, I'll play it better. That's where I get my satisfaction."

Karen: "But then you're no one in yourself. Always determined by others."

Mrs. Thomas: "If she's happy, what does it matter?"

Karen: "I don't think she's happy."

Mrs. Jones: "Sure I'm happy. I enjoy playing their games."

Cereta: "But we're here to learn to be honest with each other so we can all relax and work together. Understanding the games people play is important. But we have to learn to relate directly so we won't have to play the silly games anymore."

Mrs. Shore: "The only thing that matters is building a better world for our children. To do that adds up to trust. If we trust each other, we can work together. I think we learned that here. I think Mr. Isom and Mrs. Thomas and all of us in being more honest are able to trust one another. Now, we have to go out to others in the school and in the community and spread it around. Then we'll have a broad nucleus of parents and teachers working together to develop self-confident, creative, and productive children."

With this comment a great deal of discussion of trust followed, with lengthy comments from Mrs. Thomas describing her struggle to gain confidence and support from school staff. She concluded that the open-discussion group was a beginning and that her new openness with Mr. Isom and his response to her would bring about greater participation and involvement of community people. A major wall had broken down and the opportunity for real cooperation was there. With these comments the marathon, after eight hours, came to a close. People lingered to talk and take leave of each other. Mr. Watts held Cereta's hand and thanked her warmly for the help she had given him. All in all, we felt it was an exciting, freeing experience.

We learned a great deal from the community–school communication groups—particularly what is required in providing effective leadership. We learned, too, that we could stand by certain values only up to a point. For example, though we valued confrontation and full honesty, many of the community people were willing to continue in an encounter only to the point of becoming aware of the issues, of understanding them. Though understanding between and among persons was an important outcome, many of our group members would stop short of change or action and seemed satisfied when a tacit agreement was reached. We hoped to take conflict and issue to a place of ultimate resolution, but many times the communication was broken off before a significant breakthrough occurred. Many community people were content with reaching a new awareness and refused to push the issue further. Though we saw anger as a positive force in reducing tensions and developing more genuine relations, both community people and school staff regulated angry feelings, especially when the other person was becoming disturbed. Again and again, we realized that we had to work toward open communication more in terms of achieving freedom to speak, spontaneity, realness, and relaxation rather than in terms of honesty, brevity, and directness. We came a long way in the sense of really listening to each other, staying with an issue in a more sustained way, and not interrupting. We gained to some extent, but not fully, in eliminating defensiveness and overprotecting. There still was a tendency for some members to make extensive speeches, to be repetitive, to hang on to distortions and generalizations.

At times it was difficult to keep the focus of communication on the here and now, to concentrate on developing more open communication with the people present, to focus on our relations with each other, to share something of ourselves. These values were only partially realized. No matter how many times the ground rules of open communication were repeated, it was not possible to stop people from lengthy commentary about the problems of the school, the curriculum, ways of spending school funds, discipline, and other aspects of school life. Reminders were helpful, but as the groups unfolded and we saw the same patterns in each group, we knew that the encounter-group process was simply inappropriate with our community–school people. On the whole, they had their own style and did not veer from it. In a word, we realized we could sometimes facilitate and guide but for the most part we had to draw back and let life take its own course. The communications were consistently colorful, beautifully expressive and alive, spoken with the whole body and with wonderful gestures. Few silences occurred. One after another of the persons expressed himself with utter conviction and powerful emphasis. It was a fantastic experience to be part of sparking life where people knew what they believed, what they wanted, where people knew what they stood for and would not be deterred.

Thus, though we did not function, except infrequently, as facilitators or leaders, Cereta and I found the open-communication groups extremely rewarding experiences. The feeling of being comfortable and relaxed and of sharing freely was generated in every group. Each session had unique and unexpected elements that continually contributed to the interest and drama, sometimes to the point of putting us on the edge of our chairs. We did not follow the anticipated path for intensive group sessions, but in many moments we thrilled at the simple, profound, poetic expressions of people who lived at the raw edges and spoke with strength and determination of what they were convinced would lead to a good life for themselves and their children.

[cereta perry]

EXTENDING THE INVITATION
TO OTHERS

As a first step in the possible expansion of our project, we invited teachers of primary-unit classrooms and administrators from twenty Detroit elementary schools to participate in an action-oriented workshop at The Merrill-Palmer Institute. The following communication (abridged) was sent out by the director of Early Childhood Education of the Detroit public schools, cosponsor of the workshop:

> A workshop devoted to Humanizing Education in Primary Unit Classrooms is being offered to all primary unit teachers and administrators in selected schools. This workshop will be based upon an action research project conducted by the Williams School and The Merrill-Palmer Institute. Workshop participants will have an opportunity to directly experience the kind of activities which result in humanizing education. Staff from Merrill-Palmer and the Williams School will lead small and large group sessions during which

not only theory but actual classroom activities will be discussed and demonstrated.

The workshop offers an opportunity to selected primary unit staffs to become knowledgeable, in a practical sense, of ways to enrich their curriculum.

The group of one hundred persons who responded affirmatively to our invitation included administrators and teachers from all twenty of the selected school communities located in poverty areas of Detroit. The favorable responses indicated that we would be meeting with a group of educators interested in exploring new and different ways of being with children in classrooms.

The idea of an all-day workshop, with a relatively large group of people open to change in their schools and thereby influencing the learning climate of thousands of children, was exciting. However, the excitement was soon followed by a degree of anxiety as I considered the program for the day. I traced my anxiety to a few unanswered questions: How many of the teachers really want to be with us? If teachers have been pressured into coming, will they be willing and able to overcome their negative attitudes sufficiently to experience what we are offering?

I recognized these concerns as a hangover from my years as a classroom teacher. I shall never forget my own negative feelings in response to being pressured to attend meetings without regard for my interests and preferences. It is true that in some instances the content turned out to be of value, but since I had had no part in the decision making, I was often unenthusiastic in my initial attitude and presence.

After reflecting on my own anxiety, I began to consider the ways in which I myself had changed. I had taught in a public senior high school in Washington, D.C., for ten years before I began to examine my classroom behavior and to raise questions relevant to changes which would enhance both my students and myself. I wondered if it would be possible to offer a richer learning environment for my students. Could I be more effective in helping students assume more responsibility for their own learning? If students assumed more responsibility, would this not enrich the learning climate, encourage personal growth, and eventually contribute to the development of more autonomous, alive persons?

Whenever I ask myself questions, I try out various answers. In this case, the only answer that fit was an emphatic, "Yes!" I had gotten into a rut and it was not only possible but mandatory that I make changes which would enrich the learning climate and enhance the personal development of my students. As I struggled to find a way to effect these changes, I found myself involved in a process of self-confrontation. The areas of confrontation were:

a. my undergraduate preparation for teaching;
b. my success as a secondary-school teacher;
c. my awareness of the demands placed upon me by the administrative structure of the school;
d. the probable effects of changes in myself and my students.

As I continued my journey, I encountered similar searches by others, particularly some members of the faculty of the Menninger Foundation. A group of investigators there were involved in a study of the prevention of mental illness. They were convinced that one way to help people lead more effective lives would be to improve the social institutions that affect their lives. One of the social institutions on which they focused was the school. A central question raised was: "If the teacher understood the impact of feelings on the learning process, would he not become a better teacher? If what he taught better got across to students in an alive, effective way, wouldn't students learn genuinely, become more skilled, and thus more competent?" As the Menninger investigators continued to explore these questions, they came to the following conclusions:

> We have discovered that teachers don't have nearly as much understanding as we think they should have about the psychology of the people whom they teach or the ways that feelings interfere or facilitate in the learning process.
>
> Education has been notorious in its failure to come to grips with the feeling life of man, tending to view him as if he were an intellectual phenomenon in which all learning took place through words and books. There has been a rather general failing to recog-

nize that man has a tremendous reservoir of feelings that in many cases just gets in the way.[1]

Aldous Huxley, in a lecture entitled "Human Potentialities," [2] emphasized awareness as an absolute value of human life. He pointed out that philosophers for many, many years have encouraged man to "know thyself" but few means have been offered by which that philosophical ideal might be fulfilled. An awareness of self involves an individual facing his endowment, and searching through his physical self and his mental self to learn of his resources. He makes a search into his physical constitution, his habits of thinking, his emotional reactions, his prejudices, and his judgments in order to acquire significant new awareness and self-growth.

John Gardner[3] introduces additional support for the value of awareness and lists factors which indicate a need for self-renewal: (1) for many individuals growth has stopped and decay has set in early in their adult lives; (2) many individuals have spun intricately designed webs which make self-development extremely difficult, and often painful; (3) they have narrowed the scope and variety of their lives to such an extent that choices are almost nonexistent; and (4) more and more they take their environments for granted and find less and less stimulation for and healthy excitement in life.

From Gardner's exploration, several suggestions emerge that might enable the individual to recapture his capacity for self-renewal:

1. The individual should be helped to develop skills, attitudes, thoughts, knowledge, and understandings which will acquaint him with the vastness of his potentials and launch him on the never-ending journey of self-discovery.

2. The individual should be encouraged to develop the "how to do" orientation instead of the "what to do" orientation. In the

[1] Harry F. Rosenthal, "Mental Illness Prevention Studied," *The State Journal*, Lansing, Michigan, June 1, 1967.

[2] Aldous Huxley, "Human Potentialities." Vol. One A–101. New York: Gifford Associates.

[3] John Gardner, *Self-Renewal* (New York: Harper & Row, Publishers, 1963).

"how to do" orientation the individual develops a creative approach to problem solving as he uses curiosity, open-mindedness, objectivity, evidence, and critical thinking.

3. The individual should be provided with support as he examines his risk-taking behavior and moves to improve and/or increase his risk taking. NOTHING happens if one does not take risks. NOTHING neither fosters learning nor promotes growth.

4. The individual should be affirmed in his recognition that positive interpersonal relationships are necessary for self-renewal. The capacity to accept and to give love is an influential aspect of desirable relations with other human beings.

It was from this background of experience, and from other important breakthroughs in myself, that I came to value the human classroom.

Thus, with some ambivalence and considerable optimism, I outlined the program of the day. It consisted of four divisions: (1) general presentation and micro-lab, (2) laboratory experiences, (3) observation and discussion of films, and (4) a period of summary discussion.

GENERAL PRESENTATION AND MICRO-LAB

It was our intent that, through the experience of the micro-lab, the conference participants might begin a process of self-awareness and self-renewal.

The micro-lab is an experiential activity designed to help each participant get into touch with his reservoir of feelings and to develop an understanding of the ways in which his expression or lack of expression of feelings affects his interactions with others. To this end, the participants were invited to become involved in nonverbal and verbal activities, nonverbal and verbal communication experiences, and exercises structured to develop relationships.

A general presentation preceded the micro-lab, providing background and a framework of theory and values in humanistic education. It helped create a relaxed atmosphere and an excitement and anticipation in ushering in the micro-lab.

ORDER OF ACTIVITIES

A. *Nonverbal and Verbal Activities:*

1. Relaxation of body in space:
Find a space in the room where you can stretch out and have some space around you. Assume your most comfortable position. Now concentrate on your breathing: inhale deeply . . .* HOLD it . . . slowly exhale. Continue breathing in this way and feel your muscles relax . . . Feel your body become heavy and sink into the floor . . . Be aware of your thoughts and feelings as you lie there.

Now begin reaching out into the space around you. Use your arms and legs to learn about the space. Be aware of your feelings as you explore the space.

Allow your body to return to rest . . . Concentrate on your breathing again . . . Notice any difference in feeling now.

2. Sensing others in your small group:
Form small circles of six people . . . Move around informally among the people in your circle . . . As you move about, really notice the other members of your group . . . Linger a while with each person in order to really feel his presence.

3. Discussion of feelings toward #1 and #2:
Sharing thoughts and feelings is an enriching experience. At this time take a few minutes to learn what the experience of the morning thus far has been for each member in the group.

4. Fantasy trip—Your schools days:
Again assume a comfortable position on the floor . . . Close your eyes and concentrate on your breathing . . . Feel your body become relaxed and notice the thoughts which drift in and out of your head . . . I'd like you to focus on yourself as a child just starting school . . . Become that child on your first day of school . . . Are you excited, afraid, eager . . . just how do you feel? Who is with you as you enter the building? . . . Where do you go—to the principal's office or to your classroom? . . . Do you talk to other children or do you sit quietly alone? . . . What is the teacher

* Indicates a pause.

like? . . . Do you think she likes children? . . . Do you like her? . . .

Now you've been with this teacher and these children for three months. Take some time to get into touch with the feelings of the past three months . . . Are you feeling good about the experience or has it been a sad and lonely time?

Take five minutes and complete the experience of your elementary-school days . . . Which teachers come into your awareness? . . . Which activities? . . . Which children? . . .

Your elementary-school days are now ending. Bring the trip to a close and return to this auditorium . . . Open your eyes when you are ready to do so.

5. Discussion of the fantasy trip:

Share your trip with the five other people in your group. It is important to share all thoughts and feelings which were a part of the experience.

6. Awareness of body through movement:

Stand and stretch your body as much as you can . . . From this position, collapse your body and become as small as you can . . . Stretch again . . . Collapse . . . Stretch . . . Collapse . . . Stretch . . . Stand in a comfortable position.

Notice that the more body parts you use, the freer you become. Begin this experience with the head only. Create whatever movement you can by using only the head . . . Now allow the neck to enter the action—the head and neck are now the instruments for movement . . . Add one shoulder . . . the other shoulder . . . one arm . . . the other arm . . . the trunk . . . one leg . . . the other leg. (The entire body is now involved in movement and the participants are afforded three minutes for total body movement.)

7. Levels of feeling here and now:

Form your circles again and focus on your feelings of the moment. I'd like each person to make three statements about his feelings. I suggest you begin your statement with "At this moment, I am aware of ＿＿＿ or I feel ＿＿＿."

B. *Nonverbal and Verbal Communication Experiences:*

1. Mirroring and perpetual motion:

Select a partner from your small group. One of your pair

reproduce exactly the action of the other. (The partners are involved in this activity for five minutes.)

2. Sending nonverbal messages:

In this activity each of you will give the other a message without using words. Take a few moments to decide on the message you want to give your partner. Create action necessary to convey your message. Allow time for your partner to translate the message. (Time is allowed to enable each person to send and receive a message.)

3. Giving impressions of others in your group:

Each person in the group is asked to share his impressions of every other person. To do this, the sharer will stand in front of the individual, look directly at him and make a statement of his perceptions.

4. Back rub:

In your circle of six, turn right and sit on the floor. Move close together so that you can massage the back of the person in front of you. (A spirited record is played as this activity is done.)

C. *Developing Relationships:*

1. Getting to know one other person:

Choose a different partner from your circle. The task for the two of you is to spend the next five minutes in any way you desire to come to know one another.

2. Getting to know one another in the group through "hand talk":

Form a fairly close circle. Communication in this activity comes only through the hands. One person begins by placing one hand in the center. As each individual feels the desire, he places one hand in the center contacting the hand or hands already there. When each person has one hand in the center, the other hand is placed there. When all hands are in contact in the center, the group moves the hands in any way that will provide more knowing of others.

3. Teacher–administrator conflict:

Partners create a conflict situation which might easily arise between a teacher and an administrator. Work out a resolution. Share this with your group.

4. Body sculpture:

This activity is done in pairs. One of the pair is the sculptor.

The other is the clay with which the sculptor works. The sculptor moves the body of the other until he creates the statue that satisfies him. The sculptor then becomes the clay; the clay becomes the sculptor.

5. Group creation:
   Each group of six has the freedom to create a cooperative experience.

6. Free movement:
   While the record "I've Gotta Be Me" [4] is playing, each of you is free to move whenever you like and however you like. The limitation is the four walls of this auditorium.

During the micro-lab the entire group remained together. At the close of the micro-lab, the participants divided into small work groups to "become as little children" and get involved in various laboratory experiences.

LABORATORY EXPERIENCES

The laboratory experience provided each individual with the opportunity to gain additional data regarding a new way of being in the classroom. The following discussion preceded the breaking up into small groups.

"As you created the variety of experiences during our micro-lab," I asked, "did you construct a composite picture of the human classroom? As you became more aware of the resources valuable to an educational environment, did you think about the kind of teacher you are at this period of your development?

"Which of the following more nearly describes you?

"Teacher A is an individual who assumes the role of teacher the moment he reaches the school environs. When in this role he conveys the essence of his philosophy of education in general and his school in particular. He is a scholar who has command of his subject area and provides students with correct answers. He is

---

[4] Sammy Davis, Jr., "I've Gotta Be Me" (RS 63214 Reprise Records. A Division of Warner Brothers. Seven Arts Records, Inc.).

aware of the academic requirements of his department and feels responsible for students developing mastery of the subject matter. Teacher A values grades as a stimulus for learning and uses well-defined, objective standards to determine these grades. His classroom is thoroughly organized and students attend to the business of presenting prepared assignments.

"Teacher B is a person who accepts the responsibility for conveying the nature and essence of his own philosophy and for creating an accepting, nonjudgmental atmosphere where each student is valued as a person. He expresses himself with feeling and conviction and creates a learning climate that is personal, open, human. Teacher B expresses his ideas and values as his own. He does not impose himself on the learner, but, on the contrary, encourages the learner to evolve his own values and convictions with greater clarity and to develop insights consistent with the learner's experience. He regards the many questions and reactions of the learner with utter respect, listening with complete acceptance and making elaborations where this is important to the learner. Teacher B actively encourages each individual to be and become more fully himself. The teacher does not present himself as an authority but rather as a person concerned with the becoming nature of each member in the group as well as with his own personal growth.

"Do either of the descriptions fit you? Could you present an accurate description of you, the teacher? Are you able to say what you would like your description to be?

"The big question: How can you get where you would like to be?"

Since we assumed that the administrators and teachers wanted to move toward creating more human classrooms, we offered a series of laboratory experiences to describe methods and ways we had created to humanize learning in primary-unit classrooms. Involvement in a laboratory experience was one way of approaching an answer to the question, "What kind of teacher do you want to be?" Our students, along with teachers of primary classes at the Williams School, created activities that included a range of feelings and ideas aimed at involving conference participants, bringing about personal awareness, and increasing their ease in offering human approaches to classroom learning. A number of examples follow:

LABORATORY EXPERIENCE #1
PAINTING: MIKE AND TOM

[tom barrett]

The laboratory experience which Mike and I planned for a small group of educators is outlined below.

First of all, we wanted to get the people in our group involved on a physical level. We chose fingerpainting. It was not just ordinary, run-of-the-mill fingerpainting, however. Some members of the group were instructed to paint with any parts of their bodies except their fingers; others were told to use only their fingers. A third group was told they were free to use any part of their bodies that they wished.

We were interested in learning about the feelings resulting from group versus individual activities and silent versus verbal activities. For this reason we organized four different painting situations.

The members of Group A were instructed to work together to paint a mural. They were urged to discuss the project among themselves and to talk freely while painting. The painting could be done with any part of the body they desired.

Group B was instructed to paint a mural without the use of their hands while working in silence.

Group C had the assigned task of producing individual paintings. The members of this group had the freedom to use any parts of the body and to talk freely with each other as they painted.

Group D followed the instructions to create individual paintings while working in silence, with hands only.

At the beginning of the experience all paints were given to Groups A and C. Groups B and D had to get the paints they needed when Groups A and C were not using them. Music provided a changing background atmosphere during the activity.

After the first twenty minutes the groups were switched. Groups A and D exchanged situations; Groups B and C exchanged with one another.

Following a twenty-minute work period in the new situations, the entire group reassembled to discuss the experience. Almost every group member reported a multitude of feelings ranging from happy to sad and from frustrated to peaceful. They had experienced the differences of being in a group and being alone. Some of the group creating individual paintings experienced loneliness; others reported feelings of solitude and serenity. Those who had worked together silently felt the strong sense of unity needed to produce a beautiful mural.

There were many different reactions to the music. Some enjoyed its changing tempo; others did not. Some felt that the music enhanced the experience; others found it annoying and distracting. All agreed that they had indeed experienced FEELINGS: physical feelings of paint from noses to toes as well as inner feelings involving emotions.

Although this activity was not tried in the same form with children in the primary unit, it was done in part with them. On different occasions children painted together, sometimes with music, sometimes without; sometimes with fingers only, sometimes with noses, elbows, arms, and even feet. In every instance there was a deep level of involvement, and a wide range of feeling was experienced by the children.

LABORATORY EXPERIENCE #2 THE OPEN CLASSROOM: JAN AND KAREN

[karen shelley]

We decided to create an experience for the workshop which we hoped would allow a small group of educators to know the feeling of participating in an open classroom.

The physical setting of the room adds much to the spirit of freedom we hope the children will develop. The room is divided into activity centers. The library is situated in one corner of the room and is surrounded by bookcases. There is a rug on the floor. An easy chair is in one corner of the library and a few pillows are scattered around. Next to the library is the academic skills area. In this area is the math center, which contains a math lab kit; games to develop skills in math, spelling, reading, and logical thinking; programmed reading books; and miscellaneous material to enhance the development of academic skills. In another corner of the room near the sink are painting equipment, crayons, paste, and construction paper. One wall is covered with maps: one is a map of the world, one a map of the United States, and several are outlines of maps to be filled in and colored. Bulletin boards are filled with work done by the children. The center of the room is left free for the assembly of the children.

The morning begins with a brief meeting at which children may talk about their plans for the day. There may be announcements or mention of rules. The children are then free to pursue their interests.

The learning facilitators are available to help individuals or groups of children begin a project or deal with problems that arise. Many of the children help one another. During the last twenty minutes of the morning, the children are reassembled to assess the activities of the morning.

The workshop experience was structured in the manner described above but the time allotted was shorter.

During our final workshop period, the teachers discussed the feelings they experienced while working in the open classroom. A few people (those who were very much involved in working with materials such as the math lab and blocks) said they felt very good about the freedom they had to move from one activity to another or to stay with one activity for as long as they liked. One person, who spent the entire period painting delightful pictures and appeared to be having great fun, said she thoroughly enjoyed herself but she was afraid that if she were always given freedom she would do nothing else. A man expressed ambivalent feelings about the class. He said it was attractive to him but that he had many questions about the probability of academic success for children in this kind of classroom. This man and one or two others were very reluctant to participate in the class but wanted to talk about the pros and cons of the open-classroom concept. It was frustrating to encounter these few because the experience was organized to have individuals experience the climate of the room, not to discuss it intellectually. Most conference participants valued the opportunity for direct experience of the open classroom.

LABORATORY EXPERIENCE #3 COOPERATIVE CREATIVITY: MAUREEN AND MARGE

[marge johnson]

Various bits and pieces of the environment (cotton balls, Q-tips, wood, nails, berries, pods, straws, cloth, paint, paper, etc.) were placed on tables around the room. A tape had been made of various moods and styles of music (jazz, classical, rock, folk). The tape was played during the work period. Four individuals were put into a group to work together on one project. What they would do was left up to them. Each person was instructed to listen to the music, select the materials he desired, and create a product.

The responses to the instructions were varied. One group of four decided to use one large sheet of paper and divide it into four areas, with each person using one area. Two individuals made articles that they thought their own students could make and use. Others created projects that might be used for the approaching Christmas season. There were others who created articles expressive of their immediate feelings.

LABORATORY EXPERIENCE #4 DANCE A STORY

[nancy boxill]

"The story to be danced is Noah's Ark," I began. "The activity as structured will allow each of you to use your imagination and your body both rhythmically and freely. As the music plays, I will read the story aloud so that you can develop some understanding of this version. (Activity is completed and next step is taken.)

"Now I will turn on the record, and as the recorded story plays, will you as a group create appropriate action for the various roles presented in the story. (Activity is completed and new one is described.)

"This time will each of you select the character that you like best and create what you consider the true character for that role. (The music plays as individuals work separately on their creations.)

"The final presentation requires that the entire group form a circle. As the recorded story plays, will you enter the center of the circle and act out your role when the record indicates the appropriate time."

Concluding Comments: This record provided the stimulus for a great deal of exciting activity and the challenge to create and role-play. When time permits, individuals change roles and create new behaviors. The activity may be extended so that individuals are encouraged to design and create appropriate costumes for the characters in the story.

LABORATORY EXPERIENCE #5 WHO AM I?: MARY AND SUZANNE

[suzanne toaspern]

The project that we sponsored at the workshop was similar to one that we had done with a group of children in a primary class.

I begin this report by describing our work with the children. The theme of the project was "Who Am I?" The aim was to help children to learn more about and gain more appreciation of themselves. I started this project one day by bringing in many pictures of children with varied emotional expressions. We put them up on the wall with the words, "Who Am I?" We talked about what these words meant and I suggested that they might like to bring pictures of themselves to put on the wall. Then I read a book entitled "Who

Am I?"[5] The book was created by a first-grade class and includes pictures and short autobiographical stories written by each child. At a later date, I read the story to the children again. This time, the teacher and I asked the children to tell stories and we wrote them down as they dictated them to us. The stories were written in big letters on large sheets of paper and were stapled together to produce our own *Who Am I?* book. The children seemed to really enjoy the book. Most were able to read back what they had dictated. The big book was left on a table in the back of the room and the children often went back to talk about it. Sometimes they read the stories to one another. The next step for the children was to draw pictures of themselves. They used large pieces of newsprint and crayons. All of the children were involved in the drawing. Most of them drew pictures of their bodies; some included houses and families. There was much detail and a variety of colors in the pictures. Many of the children were eager to share their pictures with others. Some seemed shy when they were in front of the class and talked only a little; yet they were proud and happy to hold up their pictures. From the response of the children we felt this was an exciting experience and one we could share with the participants of the conference.

The "Who Am I?" project was also successful and exciting for the teachers and administrators. In the workshop we briefly reviewed our work with the children. We then distributed newsprint and crayons and talked about the different ways in which one could draw a picture portraying oneself. We put a recording on and allowed a half hour for the completion of the picture. The people seemed very involved in the drawing and worked intently, in many different ways. A few people drew pictures of how they looked. Most people drew symbolic drawings that told about themselves. A valuable part of the experience was the sharing of our pictures with one another. The conferees told about how their lives had been and were; what they loved in their lives; what they liked and disliked about themselves. I felt that people got close to who they were in just the short time we were together. They said that the music was relaxing for them and that it felt good to have the chance to think, feel, and

[5] J. Behrens, *Who Am I?* (Encino, Calif.: Elk Grove Press, Inc., 1968).

draw about themselves. I felt very warm toward all the people in our group during this experience.

LABORATORY EXPERIENCE #6 BECOMING ACQUAINTED WITH AFRICA: GWEN AND JOHN

[john grove]

We prepared the environment to include a record player, a recording of African songs, slides of the continent of Africa, and incense. These materials were used to create the illusion of an African village. We hoped that this would facilitate everyone's getting into touch with life in an African village. The African slides, music, and incense were harmoniously synchronized to create as much stimulation as possible. The participants were provided with craft materials which they used to make African musical instruments. Due to limitations of space, although the instruments were played they were not used in dances. The children at school had participated in a similar experience and had used the instruments with African dances that were introduced to them.

As the time to end the laboratory experience drew near, workshop participants and leaders continued discussions over lunch. The prevailing spirit indicated that for most the laboratory activities were well worth the effort and that they could be repeated in classroom settings.

THE FILMS

The films "Developing Self-Awareness in Young Children" [6] and "Humanizing Learning in Primary Unit Classrooms" [7] were created

[6] Clark Moustakas and Cereta Perry, "Developing Self-Awareness in Young Children," Film #1 (Detroit, Michigan: Merrill-Palmer Institute, 1972).
[7] Clark Moustakas and Cereta Perry, "Humanizing Learning in Primary Unit Classrooms," Film #2 (Detroit, Michigan: Merrill-Palmer Institute, 1972).

from ongoing experiences with children and teachers at the Williams School. As we developed our activities, the response was so enthusiastic that we decided to make a more permanent record of what we were creating. We began to video tape various activities included in the program. Sharing the tapes with the teachers and children created additional interest at the school. The children really enjoyed seeing themselves on the screen and spontaneous, animated discussions often ensued.

Then, at the end of the year, we decided that there would be value in selecting certain of the tapes and in developing a sequence that could be shared with a wider audience. One audience viewing the film consisted of the parents of children from the Williams School. Some of their comments follow:

"I like the spirit of freedom the children showed as they worked."

"It was good to see the teachers join in and participate with the children."

"The children showed good attitudes toward learning."

"I would like to know what's being done to encourage the development of the children's art."

"What's been done to have all teachers develop free classrooms?"

We were delighted by the parents' affirmation of our efforts, and with this background of experience we decided to share the films at the conference. Unfortunately, not enough time was available for verbal reaction to the films, but many people commented on them in their written reactions to the conference as a whole.

SUMMARY DISCUSSION

The final session of the workshop had a twofold purpose: to help participants crystallize their experience of the day, and to help us assess the value of the conference. To this end, the participants were asked to complete a survey. Ninety-six responded to this request; a summary of the pattern of reactions is provided below, in the form of questions and answers:

Q. What feelings did you have during the experience? (Relaxation, tension, frustration, happiness, etc.)

A. A range of feelings was reported: relaxation (65), happiness (46), tension (21), frustration (20); other feelings reported were freedom, confusion, apprehension, curiosity, isolation, friendliness, openness, cooperation, hostility, boredom, anxiety, pleasure, awareness, disappointment. Some individuals discussed the development of their feelings. In many cases, the initial feelings were those of tension and frustration. As the individuals became involved, these feelings changed to relaxation and finally to joy.

Q. In what activities were these feelings especially aroused?

A. Body movement and art work were most often mentioned in responding to this question.

Q. Did you experience feelings which you did not express?

A. Most often the answer was No.

Q. Did you feel as if you were alone?

A. A few people responded Yes but the majority did not feel alone.

Q. Did you feel you wanted to be alone?

A. Some people indicated that at certain times there was a desire to be alone, but most people reported their enjoyment of being with people.

Q. How did the music (or lack of it) make you feel?

A. The presence of music enhanced the experience. Almost without exception, when music did not accompany a laboratory experience, the participants expressed a desire for it.

Q. Would you participate in this experience again?

A. Yes—83; no—10; undecided—2; no answer—1.

Q. What changes would you make?

A. Larger room for the micro-lab; smaller work groups; the opportunity to participate in more than one laboratory experience; longer time for the workshop so that there could be more activity and more discussion; work with academic subject; more sharing between groups; observation of children's responses to the activities.

Q. What did you gain from the experience?

A. A spirit of renewal; less rigidity and more tolerance for certain activities; a feeling of unity among Detroit teachers; new approaches for one's work with children; a better understanding of oneself and others; affirmation of one's way of being with children; empathy with the children whom one taught; and active involvement.

The written feedback and verbal exchanges at the end of the day were positive signs that we had all been involved in a special, exciting educational experience.

Before people departed, they had an opportunity to browse among a group of professional books and children's stories selected and annotated by the Detroit Public Library. The books were chosen for their relevance to themes of awareness, communication, and relationships. Librarians from the School Department had attended the workshop and were able to consult and circulate the books, about two-thirds of which were taken out.

Additional resources for teachers were afforded through displays related to some of our ongoing projects at the Williams School.

EXHIBIT #1   DUSO

The display presented DUSO, a dolphin who is well known to children at the Williams School. He is the main character in a program of activities designed to assist children in developing understanding of self and others. The display presented general and specific objectives of the program; large, picturesque posters set on an easel, which are used to illustrate the stories that DUSO tells; several of the hand puppets used by the children to create roles related to the stories; and some of the colorful self-standing puppet play-props.

This display was visited by many teachers who were searching for tangible aids to foster the children's understanding of themselves and others.

EXHIBIT #2   ART CAN MAKE LEARNING FUN

"Art has a potentially vital role in the education of children. The process of drawing or painting is a complex one in which the child brings together diverse elements of his experience to make a new and meaningful whole. The picture that a child draws or paints is much more than markings on paper. It is an expression of the total child at the time he is painting. Each drawing reflects the feelings, intellectual capacities, physical development, perceptual awareness, creative involvement, aesthetic tastes, and even the social development of the individual child. Not only is each of these areas reflected in the drawing that the child does, the changes as the child grows and develops are also clearly seen in his art." [8]

An integration of art and the cognitive processes is accomplished when the child is affirmed as he creates his own alphabet book, personal book of numbers, special favorite words and feelings dictionary, or unique book of nature.

Children are free to express themselves when involved in art processes. When children are free, they are happy. When children are happy, they learn more.

EXHIBIT #3   LANGUAGE ARTS

Twenty-six beautifully illustrated picture-story prints were displayed. The prints comprise the Black ABC's[9] series and they present content especially relevant to the black child from the urban community. The words that have been selected for use in the series are those which relate to feelings, aspirations, self-respect, self-pride, and personal goals.

Through the use of these posters, the child can learn letter recognition and speech sounds. The child can be encouraged to use the pictures to produce additional words, which would mean additional recognition. He can go further and create relevant stories related to the pictures.

[8] Viktor Lowenfeld, *Creative and Mental Growth* (New York: Macmillan, 1952).

[9] *Black ABC's.* Society for Visual Education, Inc., 1345 Diversey Parkway, Chicago, Illinois 60614.

[clark moustakas]

CLOSING DAYS—NEW LIFE

WE HAVE BEEN ON A JOURNEY with children, with teachers, with parents, with community people. Our energies have been directed toward bringing into the classroom human resources which would inspire real learning. Through art, music, literature, and movement, we have created new avenues for individual expression and growth. We have witnessed children coming alive: singing, dancing, creating in pictures, in stories, in dramas, in reading, math, and science. We have experienced breakthroughs in relationships and the joy of seeing teachers as persons engaging in dialogues with children as persons. Sounds, visions, movements of human concern and human response have enabled us to bring life where there was death. We have seen teachers come to be human beings whose major commitment is directed toward seeking what it means to be human and helping others grow more fully as human beings. We have felt the glory of teachers dealing with issues and problems and searching for human solutions. Finally, we have witnessed parents and community people —initially at odds with teachers and administrators—directly opening the conflicts and facing the tensions between themselves and school people, and eventually working with them to create a healthier, more human environment for children's learning. We have observed, with excitement, parents and teachers relaxing together and learning to be free with one another. At times the climate amidst the adults was heavy and the knots became more and more pronounced, but as the struggles continued, frustration and failure shifted, and "grownups" dropped their defenses, their stiff sense of pride, and their role expectations. They learned to laugh and cry together. They learned to work together on joint projects. They created a better world, one they could believe in and care about. We experienced a new world opening up in a school setting where voices of people rang out in freedom, in joy, in love.

SUPPLEMENTAL MATERIALS
AND RESOURCES

Black ABC's. Singer Education and Training Products. Chicago, Illinois: Society for Visual Education, Inc., 1970.

Davis, Sammy, Jr. "I've Gotta Be Me." RS 63214 Reprise Records. A Division of Warner Bros. Seven Arts Records, Inc.

Detroit Public Schools. "Mathematics, Minimum Standards." Detroit, Michigan: Detroit Board of Education.

Dinkmeyer, Don. "DUSO Kit D-1." Circle Pines, Minnesota: American Guidance Service Incorporated.

First Things: Mathematics. Soundstrips for Primary Years. Guidance Associates: Pleasantville, N.Y.

Hallum, Rosemary, et. al. *Dancing Numerals.* AR 537. Freeport, New York: Educational Activities, Inc.

Palmer, Hap. *Singing Multiplication Tables: From the 2's through the 12's.* Album 45-101-6-45 rpm records. Freeport, New York: Educational Activities, Inc.

Picture Story Set 1-A: Myself. Glendale, California: Bomar Publishing Company, 1968.

Picture Story Set 1-C: Other People Around Me. Glendale, California: Bomar Publishing Company, 1968.

Taylor, Billy. "I wish I Knew How It Would Feel To Be Free." Nina Simone's Album, *Silk and Soul*. LSP 3837 RCA Victor.

ADDITIONAL RECORDS

Hoyman, Annelis. *Rhythmic Rope Jumping*, L.P. No. 4001. Deal, New Jersey: Kimbo Records.

Most children, both boys and girls, find rope jumping exhilarating and delightful. The objective of this record is total health and artistic expression.

Geiger, Jacob D. and Popper, Edwin C. *Musical Ball Skills*, L.P. No. 30. Freeport, New York: Educational Activities, Inc.

Ball handling is another motor skill welcomed by boys and girls. This record encourages the development of throwing, catching, and rolling.

Keeleric, Karoline. *Danish Ball Rhythms*, AR 34. Freeport, New York: Educational Activities, Inc.

The activities required for this record are an extension of the activities needed above. Following the instructions presented in this record will promote increased coordination, better perceptual skills, and complete exercise of the muscles of the body.

Braley, William T. *Happy Listening Time*, AR 708. Freeport, New York: Educational Activities, Inc.

This record provides a variety of stimulating experiences requiring active participation.

Palmer, Hap. *Learning Basic Skills to Music*, AR LP 514. Freeport, New York: Educational Activities, Inc.

This record is designed to help the early-elementary-school child develop his listening, motoric, and cognitive skills.

Hackett, Layne C. *Discovery Through Movement Exploration*, AR 534. Freeport, New York: Educational Activities, Inc.

The purpose of this record is:

1. to acquaint the teacher who is new to the concept of movement exploration with material which his class can use for problem solving.
2. to provide a cross-section of exemplary lessons in movement exploration.

BIBLIOGRAPHY OF CHILDREN'S BOOKS

The books included in this bibliography specifically recognize the child's affective development.

Adelman, B., and Hall, S. *On and Off the Street*. New York: Viking, 1970.

Andry, A. C., and Kratka, S. C. *Hi, New Baby*. New York: Simon & Schuster, 1970.

Anglund, Joan Walsh. *A Friend is Someone Who Likes You*. New York: Harcourt, Brace & World, 1958.

Arneson, D. J. *Secret Places*. New York: Holt, Rinehart & Winston, 1971.

Baker, B. F. *What is Black?* New York: Franklin Watts, 1969.

Baldwin, A. N. *Sunflowers for Tina*. New York: Four Winds, 1970.

Behrens, J. *Who Am I?* Encino, California: Elk Grove, 1968.

Benedick, J. *Why Can't I?* New York: McGraw-Hill, 1969.

Blue, R. *I Am Here. Yo Estoy Aqui*. New York: Franklin Watts, 1971.

Bourne, M. A. *Raccoons Are For Loving*. New York: Random House, 1968.

Brenner, B. *Faces*. New York: E. P. Dutton, 1970.

Bright, R. *I Like Red*. New York: Doubleday, 1955.

Brothers, A., and Holsclaw, C. *Just One Me*. Chicago: Follett, 1967.

Burden, Shirley. *I Wonder Why*. New York: Doubleday, 1963.

Cabassa, V. *Trixie and Tiger*. New York: Abelard-Schuman, 1967.

Carroll, R. *Where's The Kitty?* New York: Henry Z. Walck, 1962.

Coatsworth, E. *Lonely Maria*. New York: Pantheon, 1960.

Cohen, M. *Will I Have A Friend?* New York: Macmillan, 1972.

Craig, M. Jean. *The New Boy on the Sidewalk*. New York: W. W. Norton, 1967.

Cretan, G. Y. *All Except Sammy*. Boston: Little, Brown, 1966.

Dunn, P. and Dunn, T. *Feelings*. Mankato, Minnesota: Creative Educational Society, 1971.

Emberley, E. *The Wings on a Flea. A Book About Shapes*. Boston: Little, Brown, 1961.

Estes, E. *The Hundred Dresses*. New York: Harcourt, Brace & World, 1944.

Ets, M. H. *Gilberto and the Wind*. New York: Viking, 1969.

Ets, M. H. *Just Me*. New York: Viking, 1970.

Freeman, D. *Corduroy*. New York: Viking, 1970.

Goodsell, Jane. *Katie's Magic Glasses*. Boston: Houghton Mifflin, 1965.

Graham, L. *Every Man Heart Lay Down*. New York: Thomas Y. Crowell, 1970.

Graham, L. *God Wash The World and Start Again*. New York: Thomas Y. Crowell, 1971.

Graham, R. M. *The Happy Sound*. Chicago: Follett, 1970.

Grifalconi, A. *City Rhythms*. Indianapolis: Bobbs-Merrill, 1965.

Hentoff, Nat. *Journey Into Jazz*. New York: Coward-McCann, 1968.

Hopkins, L. B. *The City Spreads Its Wings*. New York: Franklin Watts, 1970.

Hopkins, L. B. *I Think I Saw A Snail*. New York: Crown, 1961.

Hopkins, L. B. *Me: A Book of Poems*. New York: Seabury, 1970.

Howell, R. R. *A Crack in the Pavement*. New York: Atheneum, 1970.

Iwasaki, Chihiro. *Staying Home Alone on a Rainy Day*. New York: McGraw-Hill, 1969.

Keats, E. J. *A Letter to Amy*. New York: Harper & Row, 1968.

Keats, E. J. *Peter's Chair*. New York: Harper & Row, 1967.

Kesselman, W. *Angelita*. New York: Hill & Wang, 1970.

Krementz, Jill. *Sweet Pea*. New York: Harcourt, Brace & World, 1969.

Lexau, J. M. *Benjie*. Eau Claire, Wisconsin: Hale, 1964.

Lexau, J. M. *Benjie on His Own*. New York: Dial, 1970.

Lund, Doris H. *Did You Ever Dream?* New York: Parents Magazine Press, 1969.

May, J. *Why People Are Different Colors.* New York: Holiday House, 1971.

Miles, M. *Annie and The Old One.* Boston: Atlantic Monthly Press, 1971.

Miles, M. *Mississippi and Possum.* Boston: Atlantic Monthly Press, 1965.

Molarsky, Osmond. *The Bigger They Come.* New York: Henry Z. Walck, 1971.

Molarsky, Osmond. *Song of the Empty Bottles.* New York: Henry Z. Walck, 1972.

Morrow, S. S. *Inatuck's Friend.* Boston: Atlantic Monthly Press, 1968.

Myers, Walter M. *Where Does The Day Go?* New York: Parents Magazine Press, 1969.

Perrine, M. *Nannabah's Friend.* Boston: Houghton Mifflin, 1970.

Raebeck, L. *Who Am I: Activity Songs For Young Children.* Chicago: Follett, 1970.

de Regniers, B. S. *A Little House of Your Own.* New York: Harcourt, Brace & World, 1955.

Reit, S. *Dear Uncle Carlos.* New York: McGraw-Hill, 1969.

Reit, S. *Jamie Visits the Nurse.* New York: McGraw-Hill, 1969.

Reit, S. *Round Things Everywhere.* New York: McGraw-Hill, 1969.

Scott, A. H. *Big Cowboy Western.* New York: Lothrop, Lee & Shepard, 1965.

Scott, A. H. *Sam.* New York: McGraw-Hill, 1967.

Serfozo, M. *Welcome Roberto! Bienvenido Roberto!* Chicago: Follett, 1969.

Sonneborn, R. A. *Friday Night is Papa Night.* New York: Viking, 1970.

Steptoe, J. *Stevie.* New York: Harper & Row, 1969.

Steptoe, J. *Uptown.* New York: Harper & Row, 1970.

Talbot, T. *I Am Maria.* Chicago: Cowles, 1969.

Udry, J. M. *Let's Be Enemies.* New York: Scholastic Book Services, 1961.

Udry, J. M. *What Mary Jo Wanted.* Chicago: Albert Whitman, 1968.

Van Leeuwen, J. *Timothy's Flower.* New York: Random House, 1967.

Viorst, J. *The Tenth Good Thing About Barney.* New York: Atheneum, 1971.

Wright, M. W. *A Sky Full of Dragons.* Austin, Texas: Steck-Vaughn, 1969.

Yachima, T. *Crow Boy.* New York: Viking, 1955.

Yachima, T. *Umbrella.* New York: Viking, 1970.

Zolotow, C. *The Hating Book.* New York: Harper & Row, 1969.

Zolotow, C. *Wake Up and Good Night.* New York: Harper & Row, 1971.

SELECTED PROFESSIONAL BIBLIOGRAPHY

Adams, Joe K. *Secrets of the Trade: Notes on Madness, Creativity, Ideology*. New York: Viking, 1971.

Allport, Gordon W. *Becoming*. New Haven: Yale University Press, 1955.

A.S.C.D. *Perceiving, Behaving, Becoming: A New Focus*. Washington, D.C.: National Education Association, 1962.

Axline, Virginia. *Dibs: In Search of Self*. Boston: Houghton Mifflin, 1964.

Beechold, Henry. *The Creative Classroom: Teaching Without Textbooks*. New York: Scribner's, 1971.

Beighley, Kenneth E. *Reading Related to Authentic Human Learning*. New York: MSS Educational, 1969.

Berger, Terry. *I Have Feelings*. New York: Behavioral Publication, 1971.

Bergin, Allen E. *Handbook of Psychotherapy and Behavior Change*. New York: John Wiley, 1971.

Borton, Terry. *Reach, Touch and Teach*. New York: McGraw-Hill, 1970.

Boy, Angela V., and Pine, Gerald J. *Expanding the Self: Personal Growth for Teachers*. Dubuque, Iowa: William C. Brown, 1971.

Branden, Nathaniel. *The Disowned Self*. Los Angeles: Nash, 1971.

Brennecke, John H., and Amick, Robert. *The Struggle for Significance*. Beverly Hills: Glencoe, 1971.

Briggs, Dorothy C. *Your Child's Self-Esteem*. New York: Doubleday, 1970.

Buber, Martin. *I and Thou.* Translated by Ronald Gregor Smith. Edinburgh: T. & T. Clark, 1937.

Bugental, James F. *The Search for Authenticity.* New York: Holt, Rinehart & Winston, 1965.

Burton, Arthur. *Encounter.* San Francisco: Jossey-Bass, 1969.

Burton, Arthur, ed. *Interpersonal Psychotherapy.* Englewood Cliffs, N.J.: Prentice-Hall, 1971.

Button, Alan DeWitt. *The Authentic Child.* New York: Random House, 1969.

Clark, Kenneth B. *Dark Ghetto.* New York: Harper & Row, 1965.

Clark, Margaret, and Erway, Ella. *The Learning Encounter.* New York: Random House, 1971.

Clive, Geoffrey. "The Inauthentic Self." *Journal of Existentialism* 5:17, Summer, 1964.

Combs, Arthur. *Professional Education of Teachers.* Boston: Allyn & Bacon, 1965.

Combs, Arthur, Avila, Donald, and Purkey, William. *Helping Relationships.* Boston: Allyn & Bacon, 1971.

Cottingham, Harold F. "The Challenge of Authentic Behavior." *Personnel & Guidance Journal* 45:4, December, 1966.

Cummings, Susan N., and Carney, John J. *Communication for Education.* New York, Pa.: Intext, 1971.

D'Ambrosio, Richard. *No Language But a Cry.* New York: Doubleday, 1970.

Dewey, John. *Democracy and Education.* New York: The Free Press, 1930.

Dimick, Kenneth, and Huff, Vaughn. *Child Counseling.* Dubuque, Iowa: William C. Brown, 1970.

Droscher, Vitus B. *The Magic of the Senses.* New York: Harper & Row, 1971.

Dumas, Enoch. *Math Activities for Child Involvement.* Boston: Allyn & Bacon, 1971.

Fagan, Joen, and Shepherd, Irma Lee. *Gestalt Therapy Now.* Palo Alto: Science & Behavior Books, 1970.

Fleishman, Alfred. *Sense and Nonsense. A Study in Human Communication.* San Francisco: International Society for General Semantics, 1971.

Frankl, Viktor. *Man's Search for Meaning.* New York: Washington Square Press, 1963.

Fromm, Erich. *The Art of Living.* New York: Bantam, 1963.

Gardner, John. *Self-Renewal.* New York: Harper & Row, 1963.

Gazda, George. *Group Counseling: A Developmental Approach.* Boston: Allyn & Bacon, 1971.

Gibbons, Maurice. *Individualized Instruction.* New York: Teachers College Press, 1971.

Ginott, Haim G. *Group Psychotherapy with Children: The Theory and Practice.* New York: McGraw-Hill, 1961.

Goffman, Erving. *The Presentation of Self in Everyday Life.* New York: Doubleday, 1959.

Gordon, Chad, and Gergen, Kenneth. *The Self in Social Interaction.* New York: John Wiley, 1968.

Greenberg, Herbert M. *Teaching With Feeling.* Toronto: Macmillan, 1969.

Greening, Thomas C. *Existential Humanistic Psychology.* Belmont, Calif.: Brooks-Cole, 1971.

Hamachek, Don, ed. *Encounters With the Self.* New York: Holt, Rinehart & Winston, 1971.

Hamachek, Don. *The Self in Growth. Teaching and Learning.* Englewood Cliffs, N.J.: Prentice-Hall, 1965.

Hawkins, David. "The Informed Vision: An Essay on Science Education." *Daedalus,* Vol. 94, No. 3, Summer, 1965.

Heath, Douglass. *Humanizing Schools.* New York: Hayden, 1971.

Holt, John. *How Children Fail.* New York: Dell, 1965.

Hunter, Elizabeth. *Encounter in the Classroom.* New York: Holt, Rinehart & Winston, 1972.

Ichheiser, Gustav. *Appearances and Realities: Misunderstanding in Human Relations.* San Francisco: Jossey-Bass, 1970.

Irwin, Martha. *Community Is The Classroom.* Midland, Michigan: Pendell, 1971.

Jersild, Arthur. *In Search of Self.* New York: Teachers College Press, 1952.

Jourard, Sidney. *Disclosing Man to Himself.* New York: Van Nostrand, 1968.

Jourard, Sidney. *Self-Disclosure.* New York: John Wiley, 1971.

Jourard, Sidney M. *The Transparent Self.* New York: Van Nostrand, 1964.

Klein, Donald C. *Community Dynamics and Mental Health.* New York: John Wiley, 1968.

Kelly, George A. "The Threat of Aggression." *Journal of Humanistic Psychology* 5:2, Fall, 1965.

Kneller, George F. *The Art and Science of Creativity.* New York: Holt, Rinehart & Winston, 1965.

Knobloch, Peter, and Goldstein, Arnold. *The Lonely Teacher.* Boston: Allyn & Bacon, 1971.

Kvaraceus, William C., et. al. *Negro Self-Concept.* New York: McGraw-Hill, 1965.

Laing, R. D. *Knots.* New York: Pantheon, 1970.

Laing, R. D., Phillipson, H., and Lee, A. R. *Interpersonal Perception.* New York: Springer, 1966.

Landau, Elliott, and Stone, Ann, eds. *Child Development Through Literature.* Englewood Cliffs, N.J.: Prentice-Hall, 1972.

Lyon, Harold C., Jr. *Learning to Feel—Feeling to Learn.* Columbus, Ohio: Charles E. Merrill, 1971.

Lytton, Hugh. *Creativity and Education.* New York: Schocken, 1972.

McDonald, Scott W. *Battle in the Classroom: Innovations in Classroom Techniques.* Scranton, Pa.: Intext, 1971.

Manning, Sheldon, and Rivlin, Harry, eds. *Conflicts in Urban Education.* New York: Basic Books, 1970.

Maslow, Abraham. *Farther Reaches of Human Nature.* New York: Viking, 1971.

Maslow, Abraham. *Toward a Psychology of Being.* New York: Van Nostrand, 1962.

May, Rollo. *Man's Search for Himself.* W. W. Norton, 1953.

Miles, Helen Cabot. "Self-Realization Through Art Appreciation." *Main Currents in Modern Thought* 18:12, November–December, 1961.

Moustakas, Clark. *The Authentic Teacher.* Cambridge, Mass.: Howard A. Doyle, 1966.

Moustakas, Clark. *Creativity and Conformity.* New York: Van Nostrand, 1967.

Moustakas, Clark. *Existential Child Therapy.* New York: Basic Books, 1966.

Moustakas, Clark. *Individuality and Encounter.* Cambridge, Mass.: Howard A. Doyle, 1968.

Moustakas, Clark. *Loneliness.* Englewood Cliffs, N.J.: Prentice-Hall, 1961.

Moustakas, Clark. *Loneliness and Love.* Englewood Cliffs, N.J.: Prentice-Hall, 1972.

Moustakas, Clark. *Personal Growth.* Cambridge, Mass.: Howard A. Doyle, 1969.

Moustakas, Clark. *Psychotherapy With Children.* New York: Harper & Row, 1959.

Moustakas, Clark. *The Self.* New York: Harper & Row, 1956.

Moustakas, Clark. *Teaching As Learning.* New York: Ballantine, 1972.

Moustakas, Clark. *The Teacher and The Child*. New York: McGraw-Hill, 1956.

Murphy, Gardner. *Human Potentialities*. New York: Basic Books, 1958.

Murphy, Gardner, and Spohn, Herbert. *Encounter with Reality*. Boston: Houghton Mifflin, 1968.

Natalicio, Luiz F. S., and Hereford, Carl F., eds. *The Teacher As a Person: A Book of Readings*. Dubuque, Iowa: William C. Brown, 1971.

O'Gorman, Ned. *The Storefront*. New York: Harper & Row, 1970.

O'Neill, William F. "Existentialism and Education for Moral Choice." *Phi Delta Kappan:* October, 1964.

Piltz, Albert, and Sund, Robert. *Creative Teaching of Science in the Elementary School*. Boston: Allyn & Bacon, 1968.

Rasey, Marie, and Menge, J. W. *What We Learn From Children*. New York: Harper & Brothers, 1956.

Reich, Charles A. *The Greening of America*. New York: Random House, 1970.

Renfield, Richard. *If Teachers Were Free*. Washington: Acropolis Books, 1969.

Rogers, Carl. *Carl Rogers on Encounter Groups*. New York: Harper & Row, 1970.

Rogers, Carl. *Freedom To Learn*. Columbus, Ohio: Charles E. Merrill, 1969.

Rogers, Carl. *On Becoming a Person*. Boston: Houghton Mifflin, 1961.

Rosenbaum, Jean, and McAuliffe, Lutie. *What Is Fear?* Englewood Cliffs, N.J.: Prentice-Hall, 1972.

Rothman, Esther. *The Angel Inside Went Sour*. New York: McKay, 1970.

Rubin, Theodore I. *The Angry Book*. Toronto: Macmillan, 1969.

Schmuck, Richard. *Group Processes in the Classroom*. Dubuque, Iowa: William C. Brown, 1971.

Sergiovanni, Thomas J., and Starratt, Robert. *Emerging Patterns of Supervision: Human Perspectives*. New York: McGraw-Hill, 1971.

Shostrom, Everett. *Man, The Manipulator*. New York: Abington, 1967.

Silberman, Charles E. *Crises in the Classroom*. New York: Random House, 1970.

Skeel, Dorothy. *Children of the Street: Teaching in the Inner City*. Englewood Cliffs, N.J.: Prentice-Hall, 1971.

Smith, James A. *Creative Teaching of the Creative Arts in the Elementary School*. Boston: Allyn & Bacon, 1967.

Smith, James A. *Creative Teaching of Reading and Literature in the Elementary School*. Boston: Allyn & Bacon, 1967.

Smith, James A. *Creative Teaching of the Social Studies in the Elementary School.* Boston: Allyn & Bacon, 1967.

Smith, James A. *Setting Conditions for Creative Teaching in the Elementary School.* Boston: Allyn & Bacon, 1966.

Starche, Walter. *The Ultimate Revolution.* New York: Harper & Row, 1969.

Sylwester, Robert. *The Elementary Teacher and Pupil Behavior.* Englewood Cliffs, N.J.: Prentice-Hall, 1971.

Thomas, Hobart. "Self Actualization Through The Group Experience." *The Journal of Humanistic Psychology* 4:1, Spring, 1964.

Tillich, Paul. *The Courage To Be.* New Haven: Yale University Press, 1952.

Torrance, Ellis Paul. *Education and The Creative Potential.* Minnesota: University of Minnesota Press, 1963.

Turner, Joseph. *Making New Schools.* New York: David McKay, 1971.

Waldman, Roy D. *Humanistic Psychiatry.* New Brunswick, N.J.: Rutgers University Press, 1971.

Weinstein, Gerald, and Fantini, Mario O., eds. *Toward Humanistic Education.* New York: Praeger, 1970.

Westcott, Alvin M., and Smith, James A. *Creative Teaching of Mathematics in the Elementary School.* Boston: Allyn & Bacon, 1967.

Winthrop, Henry. "Empathy and Self Identity Versus Role Playing and Alienation." *Journal of Existentialism* 5:17, Summer, 1964.

INDEX

Alienation
    evaluation contributing to, 12–13
    I-It process in, 11–12
    in school, 1–2, 8–12, 15–16
    pecking order contributing to, 10–11
Authentic learning
    building upon real problems, 16
    creating encounter groups, 18
    dividing groups, 17
    forming learning groups, 17
    how teachers foster, 16–19
    involving child, 18
    permitting self-evaluation, 19
    posing problems, 17
    providing resources, 17
    using contracts, 17
    using programmed instruction, 18
Awareness
    in learning, 2–5

material in developing, 2, 16
setting for developing, 27–28

Behrens, J., 161
Black ABC's, 67–68
Black children
    prejudices about, 109–11
        counteracting, 111
Branden, Nathaniel, 4
Buber, Martin, 11, 14

Clark, Kenneth B., 110
Cultural-deprivation theory
    stereotypes about, 21

Davis, Jr., Sammy, 132
Dewey, John, 82
Dignity of child
    experience related to, 25–26
Dinkmeyer, Don, 62

DUSO (Developing understanding of self and others), 62–67

Encounter process, 13–15
    grooving and groking, 15

Freedom
    in learning, 2, 4–5, 16–19

Gardner, John, 149

Hawkins, David, 16
Human values in human learning
    action-oriented workshop, 150–66
        exhibit 1: DUSO, 165
        exhibit 2: Art Can Make Learning Fun, 165
        exhibit 3: Language Arts, 166
        films, 162–63
        general presentation and micro-lab, 150–54
    dissemination of, 146–66
    involvement with twenty Detroit schools, 146–66
    laboratory experiences, 154–62
        becoming acquainted with Africa, 162
        cooperative creativity, 159
        dance a story, 159–60
        open classroom, 157–59
        painting, 156–57
        Who Am I?, 160–62
    summary discussion, 163–65
Humanistic education
    facilitating development of, 112–27
    interpersonal processes in, 119–21
    issues and problems in, 118–19
    personal growth and psychological counseling in, 113–18
    play therapy, 123–25
        creative relationship in, 123–24
    practicum experiences in, 122–26
        direct involvement in classroom, 122–23
    school and community participation, 125–26
    supervisory conferences in, 121–22
Huxley, Aldous, 149

Kneller, George F., 3, 9

Learning encounters, 50–80
    Examples of, 74–80
        Kevin and Paul, 76–77
        Ray and Marge, 74
        Steve and Anne, 77–80

Mrs. Allen's classroom, 55–62
dancing, 161
dreams and nightmares, 58
experiencing smell and taste, 61–62
favorite words, 59
listening to sounds, 60
loneliness experiences, 60
neighborhood scenes, 59–60
using stories and dramas, 57–58
Mrs. Young's classroom, 50–55
Anthony and Mrs. Young, 51–55
feeling words, 54–55
multimedia approach in, 54–55
through group discussion, 70–71
through use of puppets, 69
varied activities in, 71–74
Lewis, Richard, 54
Lowenfeld, Viktor, 166

Marcus, Sheldon, 22
Maslow, A. H., 8
Mathematics in the human classroom, 81–94
Detroit public school guidelines, 81–84
games for, 82
principles of, 84
projects for facilitating, 84–94
Dancing Numerals, 85–86
First Things: Mathematics, 86–87
measurement, 88–94
personal book of numbers, 85
Singing Multiplication Tables, 86

O'Gorman, Ned, 8
Open-communication groups, 128–45
background in forming, 128–29
example of, 129–43
values of, 143–45

Play therapy, 95–108
background of program in, 95–96
examples of, 97–108
Curtis and Carolyn, 105–8
Gloria and Carolyn, 97–99
Larry and Paul, 99–100
Margo and Suzanne, 100–103
Ron and Tom, 104–5
Walt and Tom, 103–4
supervision in, 96
Palmer, Hap, 86

Reaction vs. response, 6–7
Reich, Charles, 1
Rivlin, Harry, 22
Rogers, Carl, 16
Rosenthal, Harry F., 149

Schenk de Regniers, Beatrice, 45
Self-awareness, significance of, 4
Self-to-self awareness
    nonverbal methods in facilitating, 28–32
      breathing, 30–31
      free movement, 32
      relating to space, 29–30
      Simon Says, 31–32
      texture, temperature, touch, 28–29
    verbal methods in facilitating, 33–36
      feelings of anger, 33
      feelings of fear, 33–34
      feelings of joy, 35–36
      feelings of loneliness, 34–35
      feelings of love, 36
Self with one other
    nonverbal methods in creating partners and pairs, 37–40
      mutual breathing, 37–38
      perpetual motion, 38–39
      pushing and pulling, 37
      secret messages, 39
      statues, 39
    verbal methods in creating partners and pairs, 40–49

      conflicts with children, 41
      conflicts with teachers, 40–41
      sharing experiences, 41–49
        feeling unloved, 47–49
        friendships, 41–47
        loneliness, 44–45
Starche, Walter, 15

Udry, J. M., 45

Values in growth of self, 5–7
    active participation, 6–7
    commitment, 5–6
    involvement, 6

Wilkerson, Doxey, 22
Williams School community
    Major themes of workshop with, 23–25
      adults face themselves, 24
      developing effective behavior, 24
      values of, 24–25
    Merrill-Palmer Institute and, 21–24
Williams School Neighborhood Committee, 21–24

Yashima, T., 60